The Peacemaker Parent

Solving Problems for Today,
Teaching Independence for a Lifetime

Lorraine Esposito

Rainey House Publishing

2 Foxhall Road
Scarsdale, NY 10583
914-410-7502
www.RaineyHouse.com

ISBN: 978-0-9853943-0-1

Design and layout by Toni Williams www.LivinginBloom.com

DEDICATION

I dedicate this book to my sons, Michael and Jack, without whom I would never have understood my own personal power, let alone how to teach this to another.

I also dedicate this book to all the families who are searching for a better way to live together.

Let's create a generation of people who can think for themselves, shall we?

CONTENTS

❋ Acknowledgments

In any medium, the creation of something new is a great achievement. But it is never the achievement of one person alone. As I draw to a close the process of conceiving, writing and publishing this book, I am humbled by the number of people who have helped to make it possible. It seems fitting, then, that I would dedicate these first pages to offering them my most heartfelt thanks.

First, I want to express my thanks to all the people who have touched my life in ways seemingly unrelated. This book, and all the projects that accompany it, are only possible because of the circumstances of my entire life. If ever we have spoken for any reason, I acknowledge you as a contributor and thank you for your input. This means friends, family members, school teachers, hair dressers, neighbors, co-workers, doctors, auto mechanics, store clerks and even those with whom I've had casual conversations while waiting for a train or to be seated in a restaurant. Even if we were at odds in our conversation, I benefited because I learned something valuable from you. To attempt a listing of all your names would require a full manuscript in itself. I nonetheless thank you for your help.

There are many whose actual fingerprints are all over this book, though, and these people merit a special spotlight.

To my editor, Irene Prokop, an accomplished professional and former acquisitions editor for Crown/Random House and Perigee/Putnam and editor-in-chief for Jeremy P. Tarcher. She was thorough in the mechanics of grammar and punctuation, but also added her perspectives as a professional editor and mother. I am grateful for all the suggestions and comments that I believe were given above and beyond the scope of her initial work. In the final stage of book production, graphic designer, Toni Williams, took the lead. A fellow life coach, Toni and I clicked immediately. With an artist's creativity and an eye for detail, Toni made the layout and design of the book say with images what I was trying to say with words. I'm so grateful for the expertise that Toni brought to the project. Thank you, Irene and Toni, for ensuring my message was received as it is intended.

Special appreciation and thanks go to a few of my fitness coaching clients. During the past six years, over differing intervals of time, these women have graciously allowed me to share my journey with them during our training sessions. They began by listening to the woes of my parenting experiences, allowing me to lean on their shoulders while they offered support. When The Peacemaker Parent began to take shape, they continued to listen and support me even though, for some, the release of this book meant that I would take on a new career of coaching that would end our fitness coaching relationship. These are caring and generous friends and parents of the highest caliber. Thank you Andrea Brant, Susan Goldenberg, Robin Gottlieb, Robin Green, Jennifer Gross, Cathy Jones, Beth Kaufman, Sharon Lippman, Lauren Nossel, Kim Rosenberg, Nancy Schwartz and Suzanne Yearley.

I have had many mentors who have shortened my learning curve immeasurably. Some of you may not have even been aware that I considered you mentors because you gave your wisdom and time so openhandedly. The time spent advising me or reading my initial work not only benefited the idea and structure of the finished product, it also gave me wings. Looking beyond the rough and inexperienced presentation of my early ideas to see the jewel beneath gave me the courage to continue polishing. Your faith in me promoted my faith in myself. Thank you Candida Fink, M.D.; Cathy Woodward; Lisa Galynker, Ph.D.; Barbara Hill; Stephanie Schembari; Trent DeBerry; and Ron Mangini.

There are a few hearty souls who made room in their already crazy-busy lives to read all the bits and pieces I asked them to read. As I look back at some of my early rambling attempts, I am deeply touched that you persevered. It speaks not only to your giving nature but also to the depth of your love for me. I am grateful for your time, energy and friendship, and for your willingness always to speak the truth, even when it meant telling me something I might not like to hear. Only someone who truly cares for me would go to that extreme. I say "thank you" to my sisters, Marcelle Coder and Janine Althany, my father, David Umlauf, his wife, Anne Tavel, my mother-in-law, Kathryn Esposito, and my sister-in-law, Donna Esposito–Vasso.

Though I could have included this next person in almost all the categories above, she deserves a special place all her own. The circumstances of my life—and my life itself, for that matter—would not have been possible without her. I often tell people that I had the perfect childhood, and when I go on to describe the parts I remember most, they are astounded that I would consider it to be perfect. The times in my early days that affected me most were the years spent in poverty in Missouri. Times were so lean that ketchup and hot water substituted as tomato soup, charitable neighbors brought us groceries and our family car cost $25.00, complete with holes in the floorboards big enough to see the road passing underneath. We lived for some years on a patch of farmland in the middle of nowhere outside a town whose population was only 128. Through it all my mother made it feel perfect. Because she faced each challenge with an indomitable spirit and an unfailing belief in the temporary nature of our situation, we prevailed. I learned firsthand (the only real way anyone learns anything) that, with a vision for the future and a belief in oneself, all obstacles are temporary. Without this perfect life of mine I would not be exactly where I am today, and this spot is the only place I want to be. Thank you, Adrienne Glaeser, for your love and the example you gave me. I strive to be as you are, and that is the worthiest of goals.

The passion and purpose given to my life when I became a mother can be seen as one of those critical moments, the turning point or the fork in the road. Until this point in my life, my energy and drive were bright but unfocused; it was like hurrying to succeed without knowing exactly what success meant. With the arrival of my sons, Michael and Jack, the definition became clearer but still lacked the details that made it possible to articulate. During the difficult early years with them, my focus was trained one day at a time, just trying to make it through the day without really knowing how. As the boys and I crafted this program together, my purpose and definition of success became crystal clear and my focus began to reach far beyond the limits of time. For their contributions, enthusiasm, support and willingness to explore endless possibilities, I thank my sons, Michael and Jack Esposito.

For Michael, my greatest appreciation is for his courage and imagination. To rise every day and face a world that hurt took guts and, though he seemed a pessimist, I now understand that only the greatest optimist could ever have made it though his daily struggles. As this program unfolded, it first required all of his courage to allow his soul to open and consider the hope that lies in the possibilities of personal power. As he began to master his skills, his optimistic core proved to be the foundation that had, until then, gone unseen. Michael, you are strength and power and I know you have the indomitable spirit of your grandmother. You will shape this world in amazing ways. Thank you for contributing your ideas, courage and perseverance to this work and to my life.

For Jack, my greatest appreciation is for his noble and light heart. He has that special gift of empathy and timing, knowing the right thing to say or do at the moment it is most needed. I've watched Jack's passionate energy fortify us all time and time again. He is a giver and loyal friend, just the kind of guy you would want to be in your fox hole. For Jack, Peacemaker Parenting sparked his understanding of the personal power he felt already but didn't yet know how to define. He was the biggest tester of possibilities, first within the program and then out to the rest of his life. The knowledge that he is the master of his destiny has opened his eyes even more to the unlimited possibilities that await him. Jack, you are the stuff of greatness and I know that you will one day be the finest president this country has ever known. Thank you for always sharing fully your humor, heart and soul to this work and to my life.

Now, the hardest 'thank you' of all. It is hard only because I don't seem to have words that are powerful enough to express a gratitude that is so deep and emotional that simply typing now brings tears to my eyes. There are no words that express the appreciation I have for my husband, Ralph. Raised in an entirely different family culture, it was always difficult for him to understand my optimism and desire to think outside the conventional box. As I began to study and ponder the possibilities of physics, quantum mechanics, nonlinear dynamics, attractor patterns, biochemistry, causality and calibrated energy levels though kinesiology, he was often skeptical and downright critical. Understandably, it was hard for him to believe in the unseen; here was a man never exposed to these concepts and who was charged with the daily realities of providing for a family of four. Fortunately, in this partnership of ours, he was grounded and I was not, and both of us benefited. His determination allowed my freedom and my freedom has opened his mind. There is an old saying, and I'm not even sure from where it comes, but it goes something like this: "When both partners always agree, one of them isn't needed."

I am so very grateful to Ralph for his commitment to our family and to our love affair. He is strong and powerful like Michael and a master of empathy and timing like Jack. All who know him love him instantly. Thank you, Ralph, for supporting my quest for wisdom and purpose, even if, at first, it didn't make sense.

Lastly, I would like to thank you, the reader of this book, for considering the possibilities presented here. In doing so, you allow my family into your family in a very real and personal way, and you give me the enormous privilege of being able to share with you some of what is most special in my life. It is my hope that these experiences and insights will contribute to your own joyful experience of watching your children grow into independent thinkers prepared for lives of happiness and success.

Preface

Action is the engine that drives change. As a behavioral specialist, one of the most important things I have learned over the years is that real change requires the development of skills that will sustain new behaviors—skills developed through practice. *The Peacemaker Parent* provides a simple and practical way of teaching these skills to children, using everyday tasks appropriate to their age and skill levels. The initial benefit is a reduction in the frustration and conflict the family experiences in the morning...and then throughout the day. But the real effects of this program are experienced in a whole lifetime of effective problem-solving. Children are rewarded for working to solve the problems surrounding their morning tasks. The underlying assumption is that, with feedback and encouragement from their parents, they will succeed.

Lorraine is not a clinician; she is a mother. And when she arrived at her unique program through her own experience of raising her sons, she came to me to ensure that the principles and advice she offered were sound and consistent with proven scientific research. They are.

The Peacemaker Parent's step-by-step guidance follows B.F. Skinner's theory of Operant Conditioning in a practical and easy-to-use application. This theory verifies the premise that learning is fostered best in an environment of reinforcement and incentives. In *The Peacemaker Parent*, this environment is created by the application of a technique known as Successive Approximations. This technique reinforces correct approximations of a target behavior as a way of promoting the desired behavioral changes. This helps children learn how to make adjustments and encourages them to continue working as the goal of mastery gets closer with each adjustment.

By following the simple steps in *The Peacemaker Parent*, parents will find that getting children to do the tasks assigned is not nearly as rewarding and effective as watching them develop the skills needed to be independent and to regulate their own behavior. *The Peacemaker Parent* is founded on sound behavioral strategies providing clear and practical guidance to resolve seemingly complicated problems. I encourage parents to use this tool—and enjoy the results!

–Lisa Galynker, Ph.D.

Introduction

Does this sound familiar? "How many times do I have to tell you to brush your hair?" "Why can't you just make your bed? It isn't a hard thing to do, is it?" "You played around so much that now we're going to be late!" "It isn't my homework to remember to put in the backpack." "What? You need a flower costume today and you knew about it a month ago? Why didn't you tell me before?" "Ugh! I can't do all my things and all your things too! It's just not fair!" "You're grounded!" You're lazy!" "You don't care about anyone but yourself!"

At the same time you're nagging and yelling these little "spirit boosters" at your child, you're probably having an internal dialogue with yourself: When did everything get so out of whack? I was never like this. What have I done wrong? I'm unappreciated and taken for granted. I can't take this anymore. I can't stand the sound of my own voice! I'm getting wrinkles and gray hair over this! How will he ever make it on his own when he can't even remember to put on socks? This is supposed to be fun, but it sucks! This was all too familiar to me.

Many mornings I worried that someone might actually be outside by my house, perhaps walking a dog or exercising; I knew the madness inside my house would have been unmistakable from the street. Ever think that?

It's a deep hole filled with chaos that we find ourselves in, and it can sneak up on you the way ten pounds can sneak up on you: one pound at a time. One minute we are rolling along just fine and the next, WHAM! we're nagging and feeling horrible. All the finger pointing, blame, guilt and feelings of doom can swallow us up if we aren't careful. The only way to rise out of it all is to go back to the basics with simple and practical solutions to the here-and-now struggles that also consider a peaceful future. We must resolve the conflicts over unmade beds and missing socks while at the same time making sure that our children are prepared to eventually become fully independent adults.

The Peacemaker Parent is the result of wanting more joy and peace out of my life. It was created in collaboration with my two boys, Michael and Jack; they are really co-authors and deserve just as much credit as any other person involved. As a collaborative and personal work you'll notice that my reference to children is usually masculine and parents are usually feminine. This is not an indication of limited usefulness to boys alone; both girls and boys of all learning styles and challenges will benefit from this parenting method. The references are simply the result of the conversational style in which I wrote. I wrote as if I were speaking to a friend; if I had had girls rather than boys, the program would have been the same, but the references would have been different.

Nothing in life can prepare a person for the challenges faced by parenthood. The experience of being completely responsible for another human is the only real teacher. You and I are responsible and accountable in our parenting job, and therefore we must have the knowledge and practical tools with which to control our destinies so that we can be successful. It is so easy for other people to sit in the cheap seats handing out advice, knowing that any problem isn't really theirs to live with. Many times we are offered this kind of advice and feel obligated to abide by it, or we aren't given the tools we need to make it useful. That's why the second part of this book outlines the step-by-step method that brings these great ideas into your real life. Without understanding your options and having the right tools, you'll have a very hard time making anything better. Learning by doing is scary when the stakes are so high, and none of us want to make a mistake with our kids; the consequences are so far-reaching. As you implement the Peacemaker Parent method you not only empower your child, you empower yourself. This approach presents you with the way to apply your knowledge and intuition to create the relationship you deserve with your children. You are in control and now you have the tools you need to win. I recommend you have a small notebook handy in which to keep notes and record your thoughts during the mental exercises that follow.

The website, www.Peacemaker-Coach.com, is your home to gather additional information and to share what you know with a growing community of parents–Peacemaker Parents–joined together in a continuing dialogue. I strongly urge you to add your voice. You can ask questions, offer suggestions to others and share your experiences. Your insights, questions, advice and experiences will keep you and the rest of us empowered. I encourage you to subscribe to the Peacemaker Blog and enroll in a group coaching program that presents a coach-approach to parenting.

CHAPTER ONE

Capturing Peace

How much added joy would there be in your life if every day started out peaceful and happy? Too often in these stressful times, parenting becomes more of an unpleasant obligation than a rewarding challenge. Today's parents are tasked with so many important jobs: raising children, earning a paycheck, advancing their education and taking care of themselves as well as their spouses—if they have them. Single parents have a whole other set of problems to add to the mix.

Science has given us so much information about the human psyche and behavior, so most of us understand how and why people think and act. Renowned psychologists Carl Jung and B.F. Skinner began formulating theories as early as the 1930s. They discovered why people learn best in a positive environment and they realized the need for individuality and balance for conscious and unconscious thinking. That's all well and good. But when it comes to modifying our children's behavior, we seem unable to get the results we want, even though we have so much information. We hold stubbornly onto the old and worn-out methods of sticker charts, withholding privileges and spanking, focusing narrowly on the immediate results of our children's behavior without regard to the impact our methods will have on

If you have a lot of tension and you get a headache, do what it says on the aspirin bottle: "Take two aspirin" and "Keep away from children."
–Unknown

them in the future. We aren't considering how they think and feel about the tasks we ask them to do. Of course, those beds need to be made and the homework remembered; but besides the short-term results, we also crave a peaceful home and a happy existence in our family. Both are vital for achieving any positive future for our children.

The suggestions I share in this book outline a clear path for generating the peace we crave today, as well as for raising children who will be capable, independent and equipped to create the lives they want for themselves. I asked myself what would happen 20 years from now if I didn't give my children the tools they needed for independence and confidence. Without having given those tools to them, I won't remember what my life was like all those years ago because I'll be focused on the shambles of their adult lives. (And, as we know, the shambles an adult can make of things can produce much larger worries!) So we must be thinking about peace for the here-and-now, as well as for the future, if we are to truly have either. That's peace for today and peace for a lifetime. It means looking for new ways to discipline and guide our children. And that is why I created *The Peacemaker Parent*.

WE NEED AN UPGRADE

We've come a long way since the days of corporal punishment and dunce caps. Those were the accepted forms of behavior modification a generation or two ago. Psychologists like Edward Thorndike got the word out pretty well that those forms of negative feedback actually inhibit learning and ruin good intentions; but tangible changes in strategy are slow to materialize. Let's look at corporal punishment in schools, for example. This form of behavior modification draws from the practice of caning teenage boys in Britain during the 19th and 20th centuries. I think it safe to say that teachers are trying to modify behavior in a pretty negative way when they spank a child for misbehaving, but we have been slow to change our use of it. In the United States, each state has the authority to ban corporal punishment in its schools. New Jersey was ahead of the game and banned it in 1867, but it took another 104 years for the next state to follow. In a 2004 reaffirmation of its official policy, the American Academy of Pediatrics states that, "Corporal punishment is of limited effectiveness and has potentially deleterious side effects." It goes on to suggest that people be, "encouraged and assisted in the development of methods other than spanking for managing undesired behavior." A clear bit of excellent and intelligent advice, but what "other methods" are we to use? Without something more explicit, it is difficult to respond to the advice. Maybe that explains why, right now,

> *I think that spanking and discipline are an oxymoron, because the word 'discipline' comes from the Latin term which means 'to lead.'* –Martin Sauer

21 states still allow corporal punishment and only Ohio requires a school to honor a parent's requests regarding its use on his or her child.

For the most part, we have moved from these types of overtly negative reinforcement techniques to an era of rewards and incentives. The behavior chart, also known as the reward chart or sticker chart, seems to be the accepted tool of support. The premise is great: Rather than using the threat of punishment to stop naughty behavior, a reward is offered to incent good behavior. A huge step in the right direction, true; but something must be missing or you wouldn't be holding this book in your hands. While sticker charts have some redeeming qualities, they are not consistently getting the job done. So why are we still using them? Because until now we had nothing better.

It seems we are better able to accept and apply new approaches to solving problems in the other areas of our lives than in the realm of parenting. For example, the field of medicine has perfected so many treatments that now even a heart transplant isn't so unusual. Consider the mountain climber Kelly Perkins or the professional golfer Erik Compton. Both of these athletes had cardiomyopathy, a disease affecting the heart muscle, and both received heart transplants—Erik Compton has had two. Since her 1995 heart transplant, Kelly Perkins has scaled over eight mountains, including Mt. Kilimanjaro, the highest peak in Africa. As for Erik Compton, he is playing professional golf, has an endorsement deal with Titleist and is a new father. However, going back as little as 30 years, these two athletes would have had a much different life expectation because they could only have received treatment for their shortness of breath and fatigue, their chest pain and fainting during physical activity. They would have been treated for the *outward* symptoms of their disease. The technology to affect the cause, a heart transplant, wasn't a viable option yet. For Kelly and Erik, it would have meant frustrated lives of unfulfilled expectations and limited life experiences.

Treating the symptoms without affecting the cause of cardiomyopathy is the same as only using a sticker chart to teach a child to be an independent adult. Imagine treating Kelly Perkins for the symptoms of her disease but still expecting her to climb mountains. It would be unreasonable, right? Yet this is what we, as parents, are doing when we nag or use sticker charts that focus solely on the short-term results of doing chores.

Science has spelled out the reasons why children and adults behave in the ways they do. In the case of learning difficulties, there are plenty of examples of success once we adopt new ways of approaching the cause rather than just fixing the outward effect. No longer are children with dyslexia considered mentally retarded and written off as incapable of learning. Hans Albert Einstein recalls that his brilliant father's teachers had, at one time, considered him "mentally slow and adrift in his foolish dreams." Albert Einstein was dyslexic, true; but he was anything but mentally slow. He managed to find a way through his learning challenge to become one of the greatest physicists of all time. But what about all the others who gave up? Thomas Edison, also dyslexic, said, "My teachers say I'm addled ... my father thought I was stupid, and I almost decided I must be a dunce." I wonder how close we came to missing out on the light bulb.

Thankfully, we don't have to worry about this anymore because researchers like neurologist Samuel T. Orton looked beyond a person's ability to read or process visual information as the indicator of his or her intelligence. Through his research he discovered a physical cause and called it Strephosymbolia, or 'twisted signs.' He discovered that much of the difficulty dyslexics have is in associating the visual forms of words to their spoken forms. This went well beyond the "word blindness" theories of before. Influenced by the work of Helen Keller and noted educational psychologist Grace Fernald, he joined with psychologist and educator Anna Grillingham to develop a simultaneous multisensory approach to instruction. Years ago a child with dyslexia would have had limited opportunities or would have been written off as 'unteachable'; but today, because teaching strategies focus on the cause of the difficulty rather than the effect, a child with dyslexia has the same endless possibilities as any other child.

> *A house full of condiments and no real food. –Chuck Palahniuk*

The key to the successful resolutions of all problems is to take action that is directed at the cause of the problem. In the case of a peaceful home life, nagging your children to do simple tasks is a symptom of a bigger challenge.

I'm not suggesting that today's parents are knowingly ignoring good parenting advice or practice; in fact, we flock to bookstores, shell out thousands of dollars at seminars and workshops and spend countless hours talking to learned professionals. The desire for understanding and change is undeniably overwhelming. I was right there alongside all of you buying book after book and talking for hours to counselors, psychologists and psychiatrists in order to get a better handle on how to raise my boys. For all the time and money I invested, I received a fantastic education in the workings of a kid's mind. I knew all the theories and research behind motivation, self-esteem, self-efficacy and independence. I knew the "what" to do and the "why" I should do it, and I even knew what life could look like if I managed to get it done! Yet there was one critical piece of information that had been left out: the "how" I was to actually do it. I mean the real step-by-step how—from soup-to-nuts, beginning-to-end "how." It was as if I was expected to be able to make a delicious chocolate cake with only a picture of the cake and the ingredient list. Without knowing the measurements of the ingredients, the order in which to mix them together and the oven temperature and baking time, I might eventually make the cake but I would have to waste countless hours figuring it out by trial and error.

All I seemed to have received from my resources were fragments of the recipe; fragments like counting from one to ten to get undesirable behavior to stop; using the "time out"; talking to my child in a positive way. I think of these tidbits as fragments because they didn't address the beginning or the end with any practical application. For example, how exactly do you inspire a child to sit down to talk to you? There is a process to get that end result but the steps in that process weren't clearly defined. I often found that the bits of advice I received seemed mostly reactionary in nature, too. What if I wanted to stop the undesirable behavior before it actually started? What if I wanted to avoid time-outs altogether? Again, the real "how to" practical directions were either not clearly defined or were left out altogether.

> *Sometimes I lie awake at night and ask, "Where have I gone wrong?" Then a voice says to me, "This is going to take more than one night."*
> —Charles M. Schulz

It wasn't until I became a mother that I started to have an interest in discipline. I have two outstanding young men, ages ten and twelve, and to my surprise one started out with colic that lasted six months. Yes, colic is only supposed to last three months, but on rare occasions it can go on as long as six. I guess we won the colic lotto. (Lucky us!) My son's difficult and demanding temperament didn't end with his colic, though; it simply changed in the way it was expressed as he grew and matured. His sweet and loving core was only obvious when we were alone. In social settings he was defiant, physically abusive and the subject of almost daily phone calls from school officials. At one point I even changed the ring tone on our phone to play Beethoven's Fifth Symphony when the call was from his school because they never called to share good news. My son became an outcast and the focus of bullying and ridicule. He was nearly friendless and increasingly depressed.

I, too, became depressed and isolated. I doubted my suitability to even be a mother because I thought everything that my child did must be a result of something I had done wrong. I thought I had somehow ruined this clean slate. When he bit or hit others, I blamed myself. When he lied or acted inappropriately, I blamed myself.

For several years I tried to mold his behavior using time-outs, punishments and rewards. These were the only methods or tools I knew anything about. When he behaved badly I dutifully tightened boundaries and withheld pleasures. The result of my effort was devastating to his self-esteem and he began to call himself "an idiot" and a "bad kid." Considering the enormous effort I put into parenting and the structured environment I maintained for him, his behavior should have improved; but instead, it was getting worse.

It wasn't until he was eight years old that I sought professional help. When he was diagnosed with ADHD I began to realize that many of the inappropriate things he had done all along were directly linked to poor impulse control that is typical with ADHD. That's when I knew that the methods I had been using to correct his bad behavior were only making matters worse for him. He didn't understand why he suddenly acted badly. He only knew that he couldn't stop it. Without helping him understand his way of thinking and teaching him the skills to manage it, asking him to control his impulses was like asking him to climb Mt. Kilimanjaro with a diseased heart.

> *If you have a child who is seven feet tall, you don't cut off his head or his legs. You buy him a bigger bed and hope he plays basketball.* –Robert Altman

Though not an inconsequential diagnosis, his ADHD proved to be the easier part. At age nine his ADHD was no longer a problem, but he was far from out of the woods. It wasn't until he had a grip on his impulses that we saw the bigger obstacles that my poor handling of his ADHD had caused. He was anxious, fearful and depressed. He felt helpless to change anything about his circumstances and had resigned himself to life as an outcast and the target of ridicule. His soul was so damaged that he actually began intentionally sabotaging his chances at friendships rather than suffer the pain of rejection that he felt was his destiny.

As time passed our family life smoothed some but his unhappiness was a kind of dark cloud over an otherwise happy picture. I had written off his primary school years as a tragic lost opportunity to be a playful kid and turned my focus on getting him to college with as much esteem and confidence as I could. Helping him to rebuild his esteem and confidence has proven to be the most rewarding and challenging thing I may ever do, and it happened almost by accident.

As my boys grew I realized that the opportunity for me to begin a new career was rapidly approaching. I began to ponder my possibilities because I wanted to be ready when the time actually came, but it was impossible to think that far ahead. My days were too chaotic for introspective thinking about my future. I had to nag and nag my boys all the time to get even the smallest things done. I had become a drill sergeant, not a loving mother. How did that happen? All I really wanted was a bit of peace to think clearly and to enjoy these beautiful boys, but it's impossible to see peacefully through squinted eyes or to smile with thin, pursed lips. So I knew the first thing I had to do was to create some peace.

> *Never be afraid to try something new. Remember, amateurs built the ark. Professionals built the Titanic.*
> *—Unknown*

I began watching things as an outsider, an objective third person, and I soon realized that even though the morning aggravation only lasted an hour or so, it had effected the entire day. Days that started out easier tended to be better than days that started out frustrated. So I set about to create peaceful mornings simply because there seemed to be more bang for the buck there. Over the following few months the boys and I created what I now present to you as *The Peacemaker Parent* and its action plan, the Morning Peacemaker. The Morning Peacemaker is the engine that puts it all into action. We collaborated and put together the right combination of emotions, thoughts and actions that created the environment of peace that I had initially wanted, but we also created so much more.

The lessons of responsibility, accountability, self-control and problem solving the boys learned and practiced not only eliminated the need for my nagging in the morning; it gave them hope. Rather than feel like victims of circumstance they began to realize the power they had to choose differently and to act differently to change conditions to their liking in all parts of their lives. It may seem a stretch of the imagination to connect learning how to manage morning tasks to a feeling of personal power—but it does.

To be capable of exercising your personal power to create the life you want, you have to have skills. Those skills are the ability to motivate yourself, solve problems and control your behavior. Practicing these skills in a safe environment creates mastery and confidence. Since these skills are essential ingredients to successful independence in general, having the belief in your abilities gives you the courage to try. As Helen Keller said, "Optimism is the faith that leads to achievement. Nothing can be done without hope and confidence."

The transformation in my life and in the lives of my boys, Michael and Jack, is truly remarkable—and I'm not just referring to their morning chores; that problem was fixed within about a month. For nearly three years now I have watched as their newfound confidence has unfolded in all areas of their lives. They now have a quiet confidence about them. It came from knowing—really knowing—that they have the power to control the results in their lives. They also now know

> *Courage is not simply one of the virtues, but the form of every virtue at the testing.*
> –C.S. Lewis

that mistakes while you're learning are an expected part of learning and not a reflection of a bad or stupid boy. I watch as they approach friends, schoolwork, sports, planning future goals…you name it, using their quiet confidence. I say "quiet" because true confidence is not boastful or loud. It is a peaceful knowing that you are in control of your destiny without the need to convince others. Whenever one of them reverts back to boastful behavior or lies to compensate for a mistake, I now understand what is behind the behavior. It is a red flag telling me he feels powerless and misunderstood inside. We address the issue from that standpoint rather than simply reacting to the outward expression of their emotions.

Read the following Help Wanted ad and think how you would respond:

Full-time help wanted 24 hours a day, 7 days a week. Must also work a paying job elsewhere to fund your free work here. Applicant is required to give all her time and energy to unappreciative individuals while expecting little in return. There are no vacation or sick days included and you never get to retire. Fringe benefits include joy, laughter, purpose, pride and profound love the likes of which can be gotten no place else.

If all you read was the first part of the ad, would you send in your resumé? NO WAY! That sounds like the worst job in the whole world. Who would willingly go to work under such horrible conditions? Many of us feel that we do, though, because we fail to collect on the last sentence of the ad; we leave the joy, laughter and love all on the table as we go about the drudgery. We don't leave it behind on purpose; we just don't know how to collect. With the Peacemaker Parenting method and the Morning Peacemaker you have the tools and skills that help you reclaim the true reasons for taking on this parenting job in the first place. You deserve the best life has to offer. You deserve to be happy and peaceful. You deserve to feel good about being a parent and your children deserve to remember you as a loving parent rather than a shrieking drill sergeant. Once you begin to reap the true rewards from your parenting job you will feel like you have the best job in the world. I know I do.

CHAPTER TWO

Building a Solid Foundation

A teacher affects eternity. You can never tell where his influence stops.

–Henry B. Adams

The biggest questions you probably have right now are: (1) What is the Peacemaker Parent method? And (2) What do I have to do?

The quick answer is that the Peacemaker Parent method is a two-step process that begins with you. You'll clarify your idea of what parenting is all about. You'll figure out just what it is that you're trying to accomplish as a parent, both for today and to reach your ultimate outcome 20 years from now. The second step is the action plan. That's where the Morning Peacemaker comes in. It gives you the step-by-step instructions to put into action all that you've learned while you make nagging in the morning (and,

> *You don't DO accountable, you ARE accountable.*

eventually, anytime) a thing of the past (Hurray!). I tell you exactly what you need to do so that your child learns how to be responsible and accountable—empowered—and how to control his behavior and solve problems on his own—self-efficacy and resiliency. It's a two-for-one proposition, a real win—win for everyone.

Before we dive deeply into this whole thing, I want to be sure we have a common understanding of the words we'll use a lot. If someone were to ask you to demonstrate the meaning of "responsible," "self-control" or "problem solving," what would you do? Imagine you're playing charades. How would you get your partner to guess your word? What would you do physically to define this word? That's a difficult one, right? It's difficult because responsibility, along with self-control and problem solving, isn't an action you take. I think that's one reason why teaching these things is so difficult. How can you demonstrate to someone the way to do something that can't be acted out? Accountability and responsibility are feelings of ownership. Self-control is exerting personal will. Problem solving is a process or way of thinking. Each word describes the way of approaching things you do; but none of them is, in itself, an action you perform.

If your brain just cramped a little, it probably means you're beginning a new way of thinking—and that's good. It's good because all the other behavior modification programs that I know of approach these parenting outcomes as if they were action words, and that's why those other programs fail. You don't *do* accountable and responsible; you *are* accountable and responsible. What a huge difference.

Teaching a child accountability means finding a way to create the right environment and circumstances so that the child can teach himself how to feel positively about the things he does. As you use the Peacemaker approach to teach him to make his bed and brush his teeth in the morning without your nagging reminders, you are creating the environment that will allow him to learn what it feels like to be accountable for something. Once he learns this about his bed in the morning, the feeling of responsibility coming from within him will drive all the outward actions he takes throughout his day. Simply having made a bed won't make him feel responsible. Without empowering his independent actions and fostering a positive feeling inside him you've simply taught him a trick, much like teaching a dog to fetch. Dogs don't possess the capacity to feel accountable or responsible; they simply respond to orders. While the dog knows how to fetch, it will only perform the trick as a result of an external command. It also means that any new trick, like rolling over, must be taught from scratch because the dog lacks the ability to stimulate or motivate his own learning. But if you, as the parent, understand what your child really must learn, the "trick" (or, in this case, the made bed) is simply the vehicle with which he learns the true lesson.

> *People teach their dogs to sit, it's a trick. I've been sitting my whole life, and a dog has never looked at me as though he thought I was tricky.*
> *–Mitch Hedberg*

INNER POWER DRIVES OUTCOME

Looking at the list of parenting outcomes again you'll see that, for each outward skill, there is a corresponding internal power or capacity that makes it possible for the person to perform the skill. Your internal power makes you capable of performing the skill. While the end result of solving a problem or controlling your behavior is visible to others, your internal capacity to even try to do so isn't. The internal power is a purely personal notion of one's ability to succeed (self-efficacy). The capacity to hold oneself accountable comes from feeling empowered. It is your internal capacity that supports and drives your outward capability.

> *The essence of teaching is to make learning contagious, to have one idea spark another.*
> —Marva Collins

Why is this a part of a solid foundation? Can't we just skip to the part where he brushes his teeth without you reminding him ten times every single morning? Yes and no. Yes, we will get to fixing the problems you're having in the morning. But no in the sense that, since he's probably already mastered holding a toothbrush and moving it across his teeth, we really aren't teaching him how to brush his teeth, are we? We are teaching him how to motivate himself and solve the problems that will arise in the process of managing his time and the responsibility of brushing his teeth without your help. Once he can master these he will be on his way to meeting life head-on as an adult. Believing ourselves capable of succeeding drives everything.

Though I know you're hungry for relief now and can't bear the thought of saying "How many times do I have to tell you to (fill in the blank)?" even one more time, there is a bigger picture, a bigger prize to be had. It's important to understand the significance of self-efficacy and internal capacity right from the start, since it is so critical to your successful parenting and your child's successful life. Though right now you may think that the "how" to teach is more important, once you understand what you're teaching, it won't seem so.

TEACHING 101

Our methods are very similar to the kind of lesson plans schoolteachers develop for their students. A lesson plan for teaching sixth-grade English, for example, builds knowledge successively and includes lots of student practice (homework) and teacher feedback (grading). The teacher defines and explains the learning goals, outlines his/her expectations, provides instruction with examples, elicits classroom dis-

> *Q: Who invented fractions?*
> *A: Henry the 1/8*
> —Unknown Student

cussion and asks for practice work from the student. The teacher's feedback improves weaknesses and promotes strengths in the student's writing. As the teacher moves through the curriculum, mechanical (outward) and creative (internal) skills improve. Knowing the important role writing skills play in the future, the good teacher focuses heavily on the mechanics (outward skills), but the great teacher teaches the mechanics in such a way as to empower his/her students so that they approach writing, and all learning, with confidence (internal power).

The Peacemaker's "lesson plan" follows the same flow. You, acting as a teacher, define and explain the goals for the morning, outline your expectations, provide instruction with examples (if needed), encourage discussion and allow your child to practice. His results and your feedback improve weaknesses and promote strengths. The good parent focuses heavily on the outward skills of making beds and brushing teeth and will, therefore, struggle for years to see signs of independence from the child. The Peacemaker Parent focuses heavily on the internal power as she teaches the outward skills; in so doing, she will not only produce great outward results right away (Yay!), but she will have empowered her child with the ability and confidence to approach life with openness and independence (Yay squared!).

While the learning goals for an English teacher may differ greatly from those of a parent, the teaching plans are basically the same. Teaching is teaching and learning is learning. The best teachers find ways to empower children so they will take chances and try new things without worrying too much about making mistakes. They do this by making it clear to the child that his outward performance is not being used to judge his inner worth. A failure in spelling (or in hair brushing) does not equal a worthless person. And just as grade point averages aren't really kept until eighth grade, our program also includes a grace period: a phase of practice without consequence that is critical to empowerment and self-esteem.

BECOMING THE LITTLE ENGINE THAT COULD

For any person to be successful he must first believe he can be successful; that is a matter of *self-confidence* or *self-efficacy*. It's the prediction of your ability to do something. *Self-esteem*, on the other hand, is a feeling about worthiness. For example, a karate student with high self-efficacy would approach a new move with the expectation of mastering that move after a

little practice. A student new to karate, with low self-efficacy, would shy away from attempting the new move, thinking he would never be able to master it. In the words of Henry Ford, "Whether you think you can or you can't, either way you're right."
It can be the difference between trying new things and letting life pass you by. Self-esteem figures into this as the way a person views himself, regardless of his

Surround yourself with people who believe in you.
—Brian Koslow

abilities. One can be great at karate and still think he is unworthy, and one can be clumsy at karate while feeling great about himself as a person.

As Henry Ford said, the belief in your ability to succeed is critical to your success because it affects your willingness to try, and this applies universally to all people. Believing success is possible in one area spreads to everything you attempt. It stands to reason that you must first believe there is a chance to succeed at something before you would consider giving it your best effort, right? The ability to believe that the impossible is somehow possible springs from an inner belief in your capabilities. So how do you cultivate this root of self-efficacy and confidence in your child so he will attempt new things? First, you build a faith—trust relationship, and then you support him as he practices.

THE FAITH—TRUST FACTOR

Faith and trust are two components that form one person's belief in another's intentions and motivations. It starts to form right away in the trusting relationship he has with his core circle of influence—the people and circumstances that affect him daily. He must know he will be supported and encouraged in the right directions, and that his best interests and happiness are priorities to those around him. He must be surrounded by consistent feedback of worth and unlimited pos-

Every mother is like Moses. She does not enter the Promised Land. She prepares a world she will not see.
—Pope Paul VI

sibility so that he internalizes a strong sense of the possible-impossible. A true sense of trust allows your child to try new things that he otherwise may not think possible. What makes up for his limited experience is the trust he has in you. Without his strong belief in your kindness and love, he may only react to your dominant power over him. Sure, he may try new things, but only because he feels he has no choice, which is not the same as being open to trying new things. It's also quite likely that he will stop trying new things once your influence becomes less as he gets older.

As parents, we want our children to be happy and acceptable in society, and so we teach them to think and act according to our beliefs. Those beliefs are generally founded upon gifts we received from our parents who, in turn, got them from their parents before them. Since children come ready to instantaneously express every thought, idea and emotion fully we attempt to mold their actions by restricting the ways they think and feel, usually by telling them what not to do: Don't be stupid; Don't be greedy; Don't expect to win; Don't brag; Don't complain; etc. Often we label them clumsy, bragger, sneaky, bratty, airhead, sissy, mean, etc., all in an attempt to rein in their natural need to express.

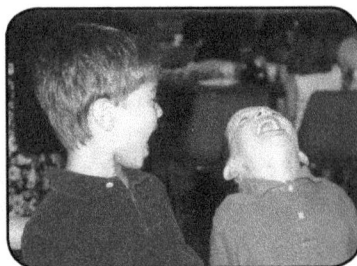

> *We spend the first twelve months of our children's lives teaching them to walk and talk and the next twelve telling them to sit down and shut up.*
> *–Phyllis Diller*

I know it's all with the best intensions. We deliver the messages by telling our children what not to do or think in order to foster the "right" kind of behavior and thinking. Saying, "Don't be stupid" is meant as "Be smart"; "Don't be greedy" means "Be considerate of others and share." Calling him "clumsy" is a way of reminding him to be more careful, and when he's "sneaky" you're telling him that it's better to be open and forthright. Our feedback is intended to help him see the error of his ways and steer him in a better direction. It's supposed to mold his behavior so that he will be a "good person."

Many of our ideas about what is proper (and the way we teach properness) were given to us by our parents and may or may not be the right fit for your child—heck, they may not have been the right fit for you either. It's a good idea to take a minute to think about where your ideas of properness came from and question them. Are they really right? Then question the manner in which they were delivered. Did they foster empowerment, confidence and self-esteem in you? Did your parents' teaching methods

> *A teacher's major contribution may pop out anonymously in the life of some ex-student's grandchild.*
> *–Wendell Berry*

inspire or discourage you? If you want to teach your child to be a good problem solver, then telling him he is stupid—even if you say "*Don't be stupid*"—isn't the best way to inspire him to try his best.

ADOPTING AN HOLISTIC APPROACH

Humanistic psychology combines the brilliance of two distinct views of the human mind: behaviorism from scientists like Ivan Pavlov and B.F. Skinner, and psychoanalysis from experts like Sigmund Freud and Carl Jung. Humanistic psychology has a more holistic view of the mind and body. Abraham Maslow, the American psychologist considered to be the father of humanistic psychology, made this scientific approach even more clear when he created a visual model of human needs. In his work "A Theory of Human Motivation" published in the *Psychological Review* in 1943, Maslow suggested that human needs are stacked in layers, one on top of another, like the rungs of a ladder. You'll climb the ladder as you satisfy each need, until you reach the top and are free to become all that you can become.

SELF-ACTUALIZING FULFILLMENT
BECOMING ALL THAT ONE IS CAPABLE OF BECOMING

ESTEEM
ACHIEVEMENT, STATUS RESPONSIBILITY, REPUTATION
PSYCHOLOGICAL/ SOCIAL
BELONGING, LOVE, ACCEPTANCE
SAFETY
SECURITY, STABILITY
PHYSICAL
AIR, WATER, FOOD, SLEEP

The bottom rung of the ladder is our basic physical needs for air, water, food and sleep. Once these needs are satisfied a person may then climb up to satisfy the need for safety, security and stability. Safety means more than freedom from physical harm; it includes stability in other areas as well, including finances, employment, family, health and property. The next rung is the need to belong, to love and be loved, and to be accepted. These are the psychological/social needs. Next is the need for esteem, including achievement, status, responsibility and reputation. Finally, after all these needs are met, it is possible to climb to the top of the ladder and focus on maximizing one's full potential.

Maslow called the needs making up the lower four rungs on the ladder *deficiency needs* (or D-needs). With the exception of the most basic physical need for life, it may not be obvious to the casual observer that anxiousness in a person is the result of an unsatisfied D-need. A person's focus will be directed toward satisfying any missing D-need, halting progress up the ladder until satisfied. And it isn't a one-and-done sort of thing, either. Anytime a previously satisfied D-need becomes unsatisfied, the person must stop upward progress as he redirects his focus to satisfy the need once again. A good example to illustrate this is the Running of the Bulls, which is part of the nine-day festival of San Fermin in Pamplona, Spain. Do you think the people in this picture are thinking about how they look right now? Are they thinking about a financial investment or their next career moves? I hope not! Those thoughts would fly out the window as they ran for their lives! This may be an extreme example, but the reasoning holds true for all situations.

Maslow observed that people at the top of the ladder tend to have good instincts about truth, are spontaneous, creative and able to think outside the conventional box: all of the things we want for our children. To be free to concentrate on problems outside yourself you must have the problems inside yourself mastered first.

THE BABY MANUAL

Many new parents wish that their babies came with instructions—but actually, they do. These instructions, however, are not written for you; they are written for them. The instructions are written inside them in a language of feelings that they are equipped to begin decoding the moment they are born.

> *Success depends on previous preparation, and without such preparation there is sure to be failure.*
> *–Confucius*

Though it's natural to think of your child as a "mini-me" (thank you, Austin Powers) since he was created from your gene pool, the truth is very different than you might think. This gene pool that created your child was not limited to only your and your spouse's chromosomes; the pool is much, much larger—think Atlantic Ocean!

To understand our context here, let's look at the scientific basics. Genes are the basic units of life and are our body's "blueprint." Genes determine our physical characteristics or traits, as well as the way in which each cell

will function. Our cells are all structured basically the same, with an
outer layer (membrane) and the
inner fluid (cytoplasm). Within the
cytoplasm are many smaller organs
(organelles). The most important
organelle is the nucleus; it's like the

> *Everything can change, but not the language that we carry inside us, like a world more exclusive and final than one's mother's womb.* —Italo Calvino

brain of the cell and contains the genetic material (chromosomes). Chromosomes contain genetic information in long strings of DNA called genes. Humans have 22 pairs of chromosomes and a single pair of sex chromosomes:
XX in females and XY in males. Each of these chromosomal pairs includes
one from the father and one from the mother. That was probably a review
of information you already knew, but just wait.

Another organelle in each cell is the mitochondria, the cellular power-
house. The mitochondria have their own ge-
nome that does not recombine during reproduc-
tion: meaning you only get mitochondrial DNA
(mtDNA) from one parent, your mother. 1987
researchers Rebecca L. Cann, Mark Stoneking
and Allan C. Wilson published an article in *Nature* with the headline "Mitochondrial DNA and
Human Evolution." Their research proved that
all currently living humans are descended from a
single female who lived in Africa about 140,000
years ago. She was dubbed "The Mitochondrial
Eve" (no biblical connections intended) and is
considered our most recent matrilineal common
ancestor.

"According to this genealogy website, I'm
60,765228th in line to the throne!"

It isn't that she was the only living female at the time, but rather that her
contemporaries either have no living decedents or are ancestors themselves
to all living people. As counterpart to Eve, y-chromosomal Adam is our
most recent patrilineal common ancestor. He has been traced to 30,000
years ago. Just as with Eve, Adam probably lived with many other men and
women; however, none of Adam's contemporaries have a direct male line
to the present day. Either their lines died out or they had at least one generation within each line that did not produce sons. Are you starting to get
a feeling about the size of the gene pool yet? Hold on, it gets even better
than that.

While it's difficult to picture a woman living 140,000 years ago, what made an even greater impact on me was learning that all modern humans, regardless of where they currently live on the planet, are descendants of a single group of people! The National Geographic Society and IBM, with funding from the Waitt Family Foundation, are currently conducting a five-year study about the migration of the human species. The study, known as the Genographic Project, has collected and analyzed DNA from thousands of people around the globe in an effort to trace the human journey that populated Earth. By tracing genetic markers, early study results conclude that each person on Earth can trace his or her ancestry to this one group who began migrating away from their central home in Africa 60,000 years ago. So if we are all descended from an original group of people, and share a common matrilineal and patrilineal ancestor dating back tens of thousands of years, isn't it possible for physical characteristics or personality traits to present themselves in your child that you knew nothing about? The crossing over of genes through the ages guarantees a unique individual is created every time. I told you the gene pool was way bigger than you thought. Doesn't understanding make accepting easier?

YOUR FATHER'S EYES

What you inherit from your ancestors are physical characteristics only; knowledge gained during life through formal education or experiences cannot be passed on. What this means is that, just as you cannot genetically transfer your knowledge of algebra or your sense of style, you cannot genetically transfer your likes and dislikes or your interpretation of happiness and success. For you to have understood those concepts you needed personal experience. The role you play as a parent and teacher of the physical world is to help guide your child as he experiences new things; but it's his job to apply his unique awareness to figure out what lights him up and to make the most of what he has.

Once you begin to understand and accept these truths and apply them to your expectations of parenting, you can begin to make profound changes in the way you parent. You begin to see your child as the individual he is and see that, even though he has your spouse's eyes and your long legs, he is unique in how he approaches the world. Let this knowledge be a little bit of peace for you right now.

Thanks to the Genographic Project and researchers like Cann, Stoneking and Wilson, it's now possible to observe objectively how all humans are physically linked to all other humans. Though this may seem like relatively new information, it's really just the scientific community catching up to confirm what spiritual traditions and psychologists have understood for many years: that we are all connected and that our connection goes deeper than even genetics.

THE HERO, THE GOOD MOTHER AND THE TRICKSTER

Sigmund Freud and Carl Jung agreed that the mind was divided into two parts: the conscious and the unconscious. I will take just a few paragraphs to explain the difference.

The conscious mind is really just all the things of which you are actively aware in the present moment and about which you could think and talk easily. The conscious mind also includes memories that can be recalled to your present thinking without too much trouble. Your conscious mind is only at work when you're awake.

The unconscious mind is on duty 24/7, performing many functions without any prompting by your conscious awareness. The unconscious mind controls bodily functions (like breathing, digestion, general health maintenance and healing), and even learned skills (like walking, talking and smiling). It is also the warehouse of all your long-term memories and beliefs. The unconscious mind is the filter or gatekeeper that weeds through all the incoming information to select only that which it feels is relevant. This selection process is based on your existing beliefs, values, expectations and desires.

It was Jung, however, who developed the idea even further by dividing the unconscious mind into two parts: the personal unconscious and the collective unconscious. The personal unconscious contains the unique experiences and memories of the individual that lie just below the surface of consciousness. Although this is what most people understand to be the unconscious mind, it is only a part of the whole; there's more.

The collective unconscious contains the universal knowledge of our species. It is the accumulated wisdom of our ancestors pulled together and passed on to each of us at birth. The collective unconscious is what we would associate with instincts. It is the warehouse of all human experiences regarding science, religion and morality. You'll find Jung's theories regarding this well organized in *The Archetypes and the Collective Unconscious*, volume nine in the collected works of Carl Jung. He uses the word "archetypes" to describe the way people have used the knowledge in their collective unconscious to form the figures that represent the basic themes of human life. An archetype is a label given to the different stages or human states of life. It might be easier to understand this if you think of an archetype as a "personality" trait, though personality as such has nothing to do with an archetype. A few examples of archetypes are the warrior, ruler, caregiver, jester and destroyer. We see the use of archetypes in ancient mythology, symbols and rituals, as well as in our instincts. Archetypes are part of the "hard wiring" that guides us through the different stages of life, like courtship, marriage, parenting and preparation for death. Jung said that archetypes were the templates used to form all our religious beliefs and our thinking processes. Even Charles Darwin, the noted naturalist and author of *On the Origin of Species*, (whose fame comes from his study of biology and evolution, not psychology), touched on this innate awareness, calling it "social instincts." They are the metaphysical, or abstract, concepts behind the creation of our ideas of character types.

You can find archetypes in even the earliest of legends. Take the hero archetype, for example. The ancient Greeks worshiped Heracles and Achilles, and the ancient Mayans worshiped the hero twins Hanahpu and Xbalanque. Moses is a hero that crosses many religions, including Christianity, Judaism and Islam.

Have you ever met a child and thought she was an "old soul"? Have you met a child who was the hero or the caregiver, or was always doing something a bit outside the box of conventional thinking—the trickster? These are archetypes and they can be recognized in some cases right from the start because, according to Jung, they represent parts of the collective

> It is important to remember that we all have magic inside us.
> –Joanne Kathleen Rowlings

unconscious. The collective unconscious has also been cited as the reason a person who has never encountered a spider or snake is instinctually afraid of them. We are hard-wired with certain things from our history as a species, and that hard-wire will invariably mix with our ancestral gene pool to create unique combinations every single time. No two snowflakes will be the same, just as no two people have the same fingerprint. When you understand how and why your child must be unique, it will help you to accept him, even when you don't understand him.

BORN TO DANCE

I got a hundred bucks says my baby beats Pete's baby.
I just think genetics are in my favor.

–Andre Agassi

Babies know they don't like to be hungry, and figure out really fast that making a fuss when they are brings a quick remedy. The newborn associates the help he receives when he calls with being worthy: "Someone cares that I'm hungry and fed me because I am worthy." He knows he loves to be hugged and cuddled, and begins to associate love and his idea of worthiness with those who hug and hold him the most. These are the positive parts of his early life experiences gathered from interacting with his core circle of influence. These experiences build his belief system. Once he establishes what he likes and dislikes, he won't really change his opinions; they are just whatever they are. What he will do, however, is begin to define his ideas about his goodness and worthiness according to the reaction he receives as he expresses what he likes and dislikes.

> *Someday, maybe, there will exist a well-informed, well-considered and yet fervent public conviction that the most deadly of all possible sins is the mutilation of a child's spirit.*
> *–Erik Erikson*

I'll use as an example a hero-type boy who loves to play Star Wars, the updated version of Cops and Robbers. There he goes running around shooting his laser (pointed finger) at his friends and saying "I killed you. You're dead." His caregiver-type father is offended by this kind of play. If his father reacts with horror or shames his son, this may cause the child to think, "I must be awful because I like something my dad thinks is awful." The boy won't stop liking Cops and Robbers; he might just stop liking himself. The son looks to his father for acceptance and forms his opinion about his goodness or badness according to his father's reactions. This means that, without a belief in his goodness he may internalize his father's reaction as a dislike of him rather than a dislike of his game.

I'm not suggesting that you pretend to like everything your child likes; he'll see through that in a minute. Rather, it's the way you dislike it that is more important than the fact that you dislike it. In other words, it's not what you do, it's how you do it that can be the difference. If you remind yourself that your child is simply role-playing in a way that is normal and remember that he will have interests that differ from yours, it will relax you.

It is my opinion that, in pre-schools and elementary schools especially, there is a profound lack of acceptance for children who deviate from the teacher's expected norm. Often a child who runs around saying "bang bang" on the playground is seen as some sort of potential threat. When the child is handled from that sense of fear, it's easy for the child to think there is something wrong with him rather than see the reaction from the teacher as a difference in likes/dislikes. I have worked hard at home to reinforce the normalness of liking cap pistols, Nerf guns and light sabers. I remind my boys that role-playing Cops and Robbers is normal for many boys and girls, and that it's the hero or trickster in them with which they are connecting. Before I figured this all out, I regrettably had allowed a lot of damage to their self-esteem to happen from outside influences. Now, when they play something that is distasteful to me, I just tell them that whatever it is just isn't my "thing," and to play it when I'm not around. It's important to distinguish a game of Cops and Robbers from behavior that is excessively violent, cruel or an actual threat to the welfare of the child or others. Excessive behavior may be an indication of a deeper issue that would require intervention and professional help. But for the vast majority of kids, they are simply playing the hero, trickster, destroyer, athlete, mother or some other archetype. If you stop to think about it, you probably did a bit of that yourself when you were a kid. It's the way we all figure out how to use our innate nature.

> *What could be worse than having climbed the ladder of success, only to find it is against the wrong wall? —Unknown*

The Andre Agassi quote that started this section is great because it's an example of the natural expectations we all have for our children. For those of you who aren't familiar with Andre Agassi, he is arguably one of the greatest professional tennis players in history. A former number one world-ranked player, his incredible career includes, among many other accomplishments, eight Grand Slam singles tournaments and an Olympic gold medal. He is the only male player to have won a career Golden Slam—that is, winning all four Grand Slam tournaments and an Olympic gold medal. By the way, the only other person to win a Golden Slam is Steffi Graff, his wife, and she won her Golden Slam in the same year! Talk about a tennis gene pool!

I can't speak for Andre Agassi, nor do I know the context from which this quote was taken, but let's suppose hypothetically for a minute that the "Pete" he refers to is Pete Sampras. Pete Sampras is also a former world number-one ranked tennis player who won 14 Grand Slam events and who happened to beat Andre Agassi in 2002 in the finals of the U.S. Open. Theirs is a well-known rivalry.

Hypothetically, let's assume Andre and Steffi create a child who inherits super-human tennis abilities and they want her to follow in their footsteps. What happens if she, indeed, has their super-human tennis abilities but doesn't have their same passion for tennis? She might be able to fulfill her parents' expectations physically, but without the passion it won't fulfill her. Maybe she was born to be a doctor who loves to play tennis. What do you do? Such an example challenges the nature-versus-nurture debate, doesn't it? It was once thought that children were given to us as clean slates. It is now widely accepted, however, that both innate qualities and personal experiences are integrated in each of us, which makes the nature-versus-nurture debate naïve. Donald Hebb, described as the father of neuropsychology and neural networks, is said to have answered a reporter's question about nature vs. nurture by posing his own: "Which contributes more to the area of a rectangle, its length or its width?" Since time can only be invested or wasted, what would you do if you were Andre Agassi and your child didn't share your passion for tennis?

WEEBLES WOBBLE BUT THEY DON'T FALL DOWN

Resiliency is key and is the product of viewing mistakes as part of the learning process. It's the ability to pick yourself up and try again, maintaining a positive expectation of success. As your child goes through life, he makes decisions based on the meaning he gives to his personal experiences. With positive thoughts of worth and capability, his decisions will be good; but with negative thoughts of worthlessness or helplessness, the decisions he makes won't. Here is the tricky part: Each new experience is stored within the context of his previous experiences. A kid who stored thoughts of stupid and lazy will make decisions that support his idea of a stupid and lazy kid. For him to succeed in the ways you want him to succeed—to be happy,

> *While we try to teach our children all about life, our children teach us what life is all about.* –Unknown

confident and open to new things—he must have thoughts that support his idea of a happy, capable and worthy kid.

I think, as parents, we feel it is our job to teach our children everything, and I think at first that's true—at least in a physical sense. Their emotional realm, however, is really taught to us by them. As your child learns from physical experience, he develops thoughts and ideas that define his opinion of himself, his self-esteem and his confidence. Hugs, kisses, being read to, a bandage for a skinned knee and a lollipop for being brave, all create the ideas of being lovable and loved. As your child figures out the physical actions that define his feelings of lovable and loved, you learn about your child, too. His response to your hug teaches you about the way he likes to be loved. When you hug too tight or too long, he'll let you know by his reaction. This is how he shapes your understanding of him. Both of you are students and both of you are teachers. The role you have in this is to show him what the world is like and how you made your way through it. His job is to take this information and process it with his feelings so that it makes sense to him in a usable way.

Red, Blue and Yellow

Your child's baby manual is as basic as the primary colors on a color wheel; there aren't many different emotions and each is bold and distinct: like/dislike, good/bad, happy/sad. Just as mixing primary colors together creates all the other colors of the rainbow, all his emotions are mixtures or shades of the basics. Making sense of life through experience creates each new emotion variation.

> *Every child is an artist. The problem is how to remain an artist once we grow up. –Pablo Picasso*

Mix red with blue and get purple, or mix yellow with red and get orange. Make a new friend and you get another shade of happy. Meet an aggressive child and you get another shade of unhappy.

Through trial and error, the child begins to adapt to situations so that he creates the colors he wants. He knows he's responding in the right way when he feels happy, and he learns tricks and ways to approach situations in order to achieve even greater happiness.

PRACTICE MAKES WISE

A person can become smart by reading books and studying the actions of others, but this won't make him wise. Knowledge without experience is just speculation; wisdom is the result of practicing and using what you learn. Through trial and error you find what works and you become wise in the process. This type of thinking is described as heuristic. It's the process that helps you

> *I hear and I forget, I see and I remember, I do and I understand.   –Confucius*

to decide issues quickly and creates your strategies and educated guesses; it's your intuitive judgment, the rule of thumb or common sense. People use heuristic thinking to link information gathered from one situation and apply it automatically to other similar situations. This process can also be thought of as Connectionism.

In 1932 the American psychologist Edward Thorndike published his theories on Connectionism and human learning in his book *The Fundamentals of Learning.* His work with cats and dogs

> *Knowledge is knowing a tomato is a fruit. Wisdom is not putting it in the fruit salad.   –Ruba*

in "puzzle boxes" proved that learning is based in cause and effect. His research contributed greatly to our modern educational psychology. Thorndike believed that learning is maximized with four primary conditions:

- *Effect:* Learning is strengthened with positive responses to behavior and weakened by negative consequences.

- *Recency:* The most recent events are remembered best and repetition is important.

- *Primacy:* First impressions are the most powerful and are difficult to unlearn, so teach it right the first time.

- *Intensity:* Learning is strengthened by an exciting teaching style and hands-on experience, but weakened with boring and rote instruction.

As your child practices heuristic thinking in an environment that strengthens learning, his speed, proficiency and confidence increase. Rather than starting from scratch every time he encounters a new situation, he applies right away the strategies that worked well in other closely related situations. Tweaking will be needed, but the basic formula will be pretty close. Since he learned to overcome an obstacle in one situation, he will learn to overcome similar obstacles in different situations, using similar strategies. He will have confidence, even when faced with the unknown.

OBSTACLES

The types of different obstacles we encounter can be grouped into a few categories:

1. *Relational:* Social interactions with others

2. *Environmental:* The physical world around you

3. *Internal:* Your physical, mental and emotional conditions

Though there are countless variations within each category, the strategy for overcoming one problem is often effective with other problems in the same category. For example, a strategy used to solve a problem with an unfriendly co-worker can be applied to an unfriendly person at your health club or church. It's the basic formula to deal with unfriendly people any-where.

Remember the book *All I Ever Needed to Know I Learned in Kindergarten* by Robert Fulghum? This short essay lists the basic lessons learned by children in kindergarten, such as to share, to put things back where you found them, to play fair and to flush. Fulghum suggests that, if adults used these simple strategies throughout their lives, the world would be a happier place. It is a beginner's list of strategies, or starting points from which solutions to even the most complex problems can be developed. When you start to look for the similarities in problems it's amazing how simple the strategies become, and it's striking how easy it is to avoid some problems altogether.

> *"Don't Hit People"*
> · *Johnny snatched your crayon*
> · *Some jerk snatched your parking space*

THE MAP IS NOT THE TERRITORY

Personal experience is necessary for learning. The phrase "the map is not the territory" was coined by Polish—American scientist and philosopher Alfred Korzybski back in 1931. In short, the phrase means that it's impos-sible to develop a good working knowledge of something without hands-on experience, because how you understand a situation depends on your opinions. It goes back to the thoughts and ideas that you carry around with you in your unconscious mind. So "the map is not the territory" means that you can read

> *The illiterate of the 21st century will not be those who cannot read and write, but those who cannot learn, unlearn and relearn.*
> —Alvin Toffler

about surfing, watch surfers on TV and even stand on a surf board on the beach, but you won't truly know and understand the thrill of surfing until you get out into the water and catch a wave for yourself. It's also the difference between looking at a map of Hawaii and being in Hawaii. As we get older, some of us are able to learn from the mistakes of others, but even that's not truly meaningful until the wave actually crashes over our heads or we watch firsthand the power of Kilauea, one of the world's most active volcanoes on Hawaii's Big Island. How could you understand the true value of warm cookies and milk unless you've experienced the deep pleasure and comfort they bring? How can you learn to accept loss without collapse until you've experienced loss and survived?

HARD LESSONS LEARNED WHILE YOUNG ARE EASIER TO LIVE WITH

To a child of five, learning a difficult lesson, like "play fair," is tough. When he makes a social mistake and suffers the natural consequences of lost friendships for that day, it is crushing for him. Learning by experience isn't an easy thing, no matter how young you are; and it's important to appreciate the difficulties and pain kids go through out on the recess playground. It isn't all roses out there; a whole lot of pushing and shoving, name calling and teasing are mixed in with the swinging, sliding and laughing. We sometimes forget how tough it is because the meaning of the word "difficult" changes relative to one's experience. For example, being ostracized on the playground one day for cheating during a game of kindergarten basketball is quickly remedied and forgotten by friends the next day—if not by the next recess—making a difficult lesson easier to accept.

As your child gets older, things start to change. The lessons remain the same, but the consequences for repeating the same mistakes become more difficult. Applying the "play fair" lesson to a college student cheating on an exam can have very serious consequences that aren't so easily and quickly remedied. How about the adult who cheats on his income tax or lies to her investors while she pockets their money? The consequences become increasingly severe, while the basic lesson remains the same: *Play fair.*

The importance of allowing the space for trial and error early in life is crucial. We now understand that wisdom can only truly come by personal experience. If a child doesn't experience the lessons of playing fair with others early in life—say his parents always bailed him out of the difficult consequences of his actions or molded ethics to justify unethical situations—the child is likely to learn a lesson that will not serve him well as an adult. Just read any newspaper and you'll find plenty of examples of people who did not learn critical lessons early enough to prevent the damage they caused to themselves and others. So the bottom line with this is to allow your children the freedom to try, to fail and to try again, by supporting them as they make their mistakes. That's what I call supportive empowerment, and it's the "training wheels" part of the Peacemaker Parent method.

TRUST AND FAITH

Every deep relationship is based in trust and faith. Though the words are synonyms, they are subtly distinct in the feelings they produce in us. *Trust* is a relationship of reliance while *faith* is a belief in the trustworthiness of a person. While trust doesn't require a belief in the good character of the other person (criminals will trust each other to some degree), faith, on the other hand, suggests a belief in the other person's good intensions. Both trust and faith are used to predict the outcome of the future events. Trust is slanted more toward the actions of another person—such as keeping a promise—and faith describes the motivation that led to the action—such as having someone's best interests at heart. For me, trust is belief in the tangible and objective, things you can verify with your five senses. Faith, on the other hand, is belief in the unseen. Faith is felt and verified by your heart. I believe you can have trust without faith, but you cannot have faith without trust.

Faith–trust is standard equipment that comes with every child because he has no ability to doubt the information given to him by his parents. He accepts everything on faith because he believes in his parents' honesty, good intentions and competence. All the information the child receives early on establishes his unconscious gatekeeper. From then on only those ideas that match are allowed in and all new experiences are measured against this programming. It is the only way that the child can understand and make use of new information.

As adults, we have the option to stick with the early programming given to us by our parents or to modify what may have been inaccurate to form a new structural foundation. Modifying early programming isn't such an easy thing to do, however. Most of the early gifts given to us have long since been filed away in our unconscious minds and are no longer even noticed consciously. Since all new incoming data must initially pass our unconscious gatekeeper, it's critical to reinforce confidence and self-worth early. A child will need a liberal gatekeeper to allow for his unlimited possibilities and enable him to explore his unlimited potential. With a gatekeeper that allows the possibility of accomplishment and a faith in himself, there is no limit to the achievements he can make.

James S. Coleman, an American sociologist, proposes in his book *Foundations of Social Theory* that trust promotes actions even when there is a lack of information. He also writes that there is a time delay between feelings of trust and the outward actions of reliance. Coleman concludes that power and the position of dependence affect the true nature of trust. He believes that one who is dependent on another can't actually trust the other in a moral sense, but only reacts to the other person's power over him. I think Coleman must have been writing about older children and adults, because I believe that babies and young children trust differently.

A baby gives you his faith–trust even though he is in the dependent role to your power position, because he is initially unaware that his position is one of dependence. Heck, it took a few months for him to even distinguish you as a separate entity. He believes completely in your good intentions, honesty and competence. As he gets older, he begins to develop a separate sense of himself; when inconsistencies arise, he will begin to question many things he once took for granted. For example, he becomes at odds with you over eating Brussels sprouts versus chocolate cake for dinner. He believes it is in his best

> *Children are unpredictable. You never know what inconsistency they're going to catch you in next. –Franklin P. Jones*

interest to eat chocolate cake because...well...need I say more? You, on the other hand, know chocolate cake is not going to provide the essential elements he needs to grow and...again, need I say more? This presents an inconsistency for him. Before now he believed that you wanted for him all the things that make him happy. But Brussels sprouts aren't going to make him happy and you know it, so what's up? He goes along with your Brussels sprouts at dinner, but it is based more on your power position than his conviction. As he experiences more and more inconsistencies, he may begin to change his unconditional faith–trust. Your position of power requires his compliance, but the faith component will begin to change.

THE GAP WIDENS

How does this dissolution of his faith manifest itself? Your child will begin to question your motives and think that you don't "get it." He'll think you are pulling in the opposite direction and care nothing for his happiness. While trust broken due to incompetence is more readily mended, failing to fulfill the belief in good intentions and honesty means a quick death to faith. Mending this break requires an almost complete restart. Therefore, being and acting trustworthy are critical to maintaining your child's faith–trust. He must know you understand his feelings and desires and that you also see those feelings and desires as high priorities. Your child must believe you truly want to help him find happiness.

NOW VS. LATER

As parents we tend to have a longer-range view of happiness. When we require our children to study for tests and get good grades in school, it is to ensure an adulthood of happiness and great opportunities. The happiness we are helping them work towards is years away.

Your child, on the other hand, though also very interested in happiness, tends to only see two feet in front of his face. He wants to be happy now and to go play with his friends now! When you require him to prioritize study over play, you are at odds with his understanding of happiness. It's those darn Brussels sprouts all over again. In this instance, his faith that you truly have his desires and priorities in mind at all times will come in very handy to ease his frustration with you. If he believes that you want for him the immediate happiness of play just as he does, he will listen more openly to your decision about studying instead. You'll still require him to study and he'll still not like it, but perhaps there is a compromise so that each of you satisfies your mandates.

You may think that your child trusts your word about things that are unknown to him and that he believes what you say. I'd say "yes and no" to that. He will take your word as truth, but his faith might not be satisfied unless he has the deep belief that you understand him and his feelings. Without faith on the subjective level he will have greater anxiety about what you say and will continue to test and pull in the opposite direction.

Here is another example, using homework and television. It's after school on a Monday and your sixth-grader comes home with tons of homework. He is exhausted from his day and plops down in front of the TV. After you review his backpack and see the amount of work to be done and the limited time in which to do it all, you walk over to the TV and stand in his line of sight while you talk to him about his homework. As you talk, it's obvious he isn't listening. You try talking louder and with more emotion to capture his attention, and finally turn off the TV and start scolding. This is a tricky situation that has disaster written all over it. You're angry with him for several reasons: not listening to you, not seeming to care about his homework, not being motivated. You feel the burden of his homework is on you; the obligation to see him through primary school seems daunting; you become frustrated and realize you'll need to spend another late evening attending to him and his homework. You feel hurt, rushed, stressed, unappreciated, used and taken for granted.

He is angry for several reasons as well. He feels pressured from a stressful day at school, where his teachers are always pushing; pressured by so much homework waiting for him; anxious over not understanding some of the math he has to face tonight; hurt over peer interactions he had at school; angry because he's never allowed to just relax his body and brain for a while; frustrated over always having to miss the program he likes; angry that he seems to have to "work" all the time while his friends seem always to get to goof-off; angry that nothing he does is ever enough for you. He is hungry, tired, pressured, frustrated, scared and misunderstood.

The objective facts of the situation are:

There is at least 2 hours of homework to do	2 hrs.
Little League practice takes 2½ hours, including travel and shower time	2.5 hrs.
Dinner takes 1½ hours, including your kitchen clean-up	1.5 hrs.
Total Time Needed	6 hrs
The time is now 3:00 and bedtime is 9:30, leaving 6½ hours for just the basics	6.5 hrs.
There is only ½ hour for anything else tonight	0.5 hr. available

Boy this is pressure! Pressure on you both! What do you do when your agendas are at odds? This is where faith–trust comes in. If your child believes that you truly understand how he feels, he will open and relax. At the very least, he will be less confrontational because he'll see that you are as frustrated by the situation as he is. If he feels that you are as disappointed in the small amount of free time he has tonight, he will see you as a comrade, not an enemy. You treat your comrades much differently than your enemies, even when you disagree with your comrades. The thread of faith will make a confrontational situation one of unified forces working to get through this together. The delicate thread of faith is extremely strong when applied to a situation like this. It can pull mountains together and hold ships at the dock in even the most torrential hurricane. But at the same time, it is the most difficult to create and oh-so-fragile when not maintained and prioritized.

> *I destroy my enemies when I make them my friends.*
> *–Abraham Lincoln*

It is well documented in psychology that children raised in trusting, accepting and loving environments have a better ability to trust others and even themselves. They are more likely to stretch their limits, knowing they have support at home. Building trust at home creates the family's social capital too, which is essential for you as a parent in order to have social influence with your child. The greater the faith—trust he has in you, the easier it will be to influence him as he makes decisions now and throughout his life. A healthy supply of social capital may make all the difference when peer pressure comes a calling.

An Environment of Trust

Earlier I talked about three primary types of problems: relational, environmental and personal. All of these problems also relate directly to trust. A child must trust in his relationships with others, he must trust in his environment and he must trust in himself. We've talked about relational trust, and it relates directly to personal trust as well; but environmental trust? What could that mean? Aside from trusting that you are free from harm in your environment, there is another element to environmental trust that increases motivation and productivity. Remember, safety is the second rung on the ladder of needs, according to Maslow, and must be satisfied before moving up. Establishing a structure and organization in your home will create feelings of trust and security in your child. Life is stressful and often chaotic, so maintaining a structure and order to your child's daily routine will reduce anxiety and increase cooperation. Remember, all the basic needs must be met for a child to branch out and try new things. The Peacemaker Parent method gives you an exact way to establish an environment in the morning that will increase a feeling of environmental trust, peace and cooperation.

Why the morning and not the afternoon or evening? I've had many friends ask me to first fix the "witching hour" (the hour or so before dinner) or the homework "hell-time." While I totally understand the extreme need for help at these times (I've had my share of the pain, too), I believe the only way to fix them is by fixing the morning first. The morning has fewer unexpected hiccups that can derail even the best of plans. There are many things outside your control that can accumulate during the day. The morning, however, is fairly straightforward and routine. It will be easier for you to established peace in the morning and then stand back and watch how it flows out to the other parts of the day as well. As for me, I don't have nearly the issues over homework that I had before. It isn't that my boys miraculously saw the benefit of doing their homework. Hardly! The difference is that, while they still think it's pointless, they know it is their responsibility to do it. They learned what responsibility felt like by being responsible for their morning chores, and that feeling has caught on.

Choice Theory

Over a 50-year period, the noted American psychologist William Glasser, MD developed what is now called Choice Theory and, in 1998, published the book *Choice Theory: A New Psychology of Personal Freedom*. Similar to Maslow's humanistic psychology, Glasser believes that behavior is driven by a set of physical and psychological needs that are the result of our idea of a "quality world"—a world that contains the values, people and things we hold most dear. He believes our actions are all directed towards making the physical world match as closely as possible to our idea of this quality world. According to Choice Theory, behavior is thinking, acting, feeling and physiology—your body at work. Choice theorists believe individuals have a great degree of control over the first two and little ability to directly control feeling and the body. It is their belief that, by controlling our choices in thinking and acting, we indirectly influence our feelings and physiology. I'm not so sure. Consider that your thoughts and actions are part of your conscious mind, and your feelings and body are controlled by your unconscious mind. Since your unconscious mind is the gatekeeper that directs your conscious mind, can we really expect that all behavior can be consciously controlled? We expect our children to have greater control over their thoughts and actions than maybe they really can have, and so we are often disappointed when they choose poorly over and over again.

It seems as if it should be so easy to simply make up our minds to do something and then do it, right? But if this were true then all our New Year's resolutions would be met. Take losing weight, for example:

- You consciously decided to lose weight;

- You controlled your thoughts and actions consciously;

- You didn't lose weight. Why not?

Your unconscious programming sends messages like *I'm not good enough; I'm weak; It'll never work.* Guess what happens: You and the other 93% who resolved to lose weight not only regain what was lost, but you'll probably add an extra two pounds to boot! I believe that, if emotions are not in line with conscious choices from the start, changes may only be temporary, at best. It is the unconscious mind that moves the body into action; it is the unconscious mind that has registered all the early teachings about goodness, ability and worth. The unconscious mind is the gateway through which all information is processed and, therefore, it greatly affects the conscious choices we make.

While I agree that we have conscious control over our thoughts and actions, I also believe that success cannot be sustained if emotions are not in line with the way in which we want to think and act. That's why it is so important to understand all these things before we begin to look at the specific actions of the Morning Peacemaker. Without the underlying understanding of how things work, the motions you go through won't yield the lasting results that you and your child deserve.

THE FLIP SIDE

Let's think about the flip side of all this. What would be the result of an environment that does not promote empowerment, confidence and self-esteem? For starters, your stressful mornings, anger, frustration, doubt and hopelessness would continue to grow, keeping you from the relationship you deserve with your child. What about your child? Sure, you'll have doubts about his ability to take care of himself later on, but there is an even greater threat present that could hold him back and limit his potential even more.

In 1967 Martin Seligman, an American psychologist who is a world-renowned expert on depression and abnormal psychology, first discovered Learned Helplessness Theory by accident while he was researching depression at the University of Pennsylvania. Many animal experiments followed, using the avoidance response of dogs and rats when exposed to electrical shock. In an experiment conducted by Steven Maier (University of Colorado Distinguished Professor and the Director of the Center for Neuroscience) dogs were placed in separate cages and were given electric shocks through the floor of the cage. The dogs had no way to escape the painful electric shock. After the dogs became resigned to their fate and curled up whimpering, the shock was eliminated on half of the cage. The scientists then dragged the dogs to the safe area, showing them the way out. What do you think the dogs did? It seems logical that the dogs would remain on the safe side, right? Wrong. The dogs had learned to be helpless when they became resigned to their fate and to the pain. When the researchers let them go, the dogs went right back to the shock side of the cage and curled up once again in fear. This is the same sort of behavior you'll see in a child who has given up trying.

The news is not all bleak, however, because this condition can be un-learned over time. How long do you think it took those dogs to unlearn their helplessness? How many times would they need to have been dragged to the safe side before they became aware of their power to escape on their own? Would they need to be dragged three times, seven times, fifteen times? Keep going. The dogs needed to be dragged thirty to fifty times before they began to act on their own! Thirty to fifty times! Amazing! Humans aren't much different; just visit any shelter for abused women and you'll know.

I'm not suggesting children will develop debilitating chronic helplessness if not taught how to manage their time in the morning well enough to brush their teeth and make their beds. What might happen, though, is that learned helplessness in other parts of the child's life may affect his ability to be in-dependent at home. When your child is away from home (like at school or camp) he may encounter environments that cause feelings of anxiety, distress and chaos. What about his experience with bullies, teachers who in-timidate, coaches who shame, clergy who use fear of retribution as a means to mold behavior? What about all the other adults who have an expressed role of authority, or all other peers who dominate physically or emotion-ally? You cannot prevent many of these situations. You can't go to school with your child, so you can't know for sure how your son's teacher behaves in the classroom. Fortunately, the vast majority of teachers are outstand-ing and nurturing; but there are some who aren't. One of my sons had an elementary teacher who actually said to the class, "You are the worst class I have ever had!" Do you think that empowered the class or did it cause stress, anxiety and underperformance? Coaches who are passionate about their game can shame players, even if they aren't aware of the impact their words have. "How could you miss that easy shot? Haven't you been prac-ticing? We lost the game because of you!" Or how about that kid at school who decides to pick on your son? Schools are getting better at helping to eliminate bullying through awareness programs, peer mediation and coun-seling, but it is still very much in evidence. When another child intimidates your son every day at school, and the system isn't doing enough to protect him, he may become resigned to his fate and begin to expect it. He could begin to feel like an outcast or target and learn to behave like one. Ugh!

As a Peacemaker Parent using the Morning Peacemaker program, and through the supported empowerment and open communication that this provides, you teach your child how to take control and help himself. It allows him the opportunity to practice solving problems in a safe and supportive environment so that he begins to understand his power. Once he masters his morning, he'll begin to use his skills elsewhere and will no longer accept circumstances that don't serve him. He will become the master of his destiny and will never again allow outside forces to determine his results. YAY!

CHAPTER THREE

Set Your Sights

It is more important to know where you are going than to get there quickly. Do not mistake activity for achievement.

—Mabel Newcomber

Before beginning anything new, it's important to have a clearly defined objective. As Yogi Berra said, "If you don't know where you're going, you could end up someplace else." So what exactly are you trying to accomplish? What is your objective?

If you still answer that your objective is to get out of the house in the morning on time without nagging your kids, I'll deliver the answer right now. Here's what you do: Wake your kids in the morning, and tell them to get ready for the day and to meet you at the door when it's time to go. Let them do their morning chores on their own and be willing to accept whatever meets you at the door. Nagging isn't required if you accept that teeth and hair don't get brushed, or that beds didn't get made, or proper street clothes aren't worn. You just wake up in the morning and go about your routine while letting your kids go about their routines. There—you have your objective. Happy? No?

You obviously want more than just getting out in the morning without hassles. So think about this again. What are your true objectives? You probably want peace and harmony in your morning and throughout your day. You want to go into your day happy, knowing that everything at home is running smoothly and that your children are learning to be independent and responsible. You want mutual trust and respect. You want your children to approach life with an indomitable spirit because they know that they can do anything they put their minds to. You want them to have high self-esteem so that little bumps along the road won't discourage them from trying new things. You want them to remain open to all the wonders of the world. At first this seems to be a far cry from simply getting out the door in the morning without nagging. Aren't they completely different objectives altogether? No, not really.

Clouds

When we are sure that we are on the right road there is no need to plan our journey too far ahead. No need to burden ourselves with doubts and fears as to the obstacles that may bar our progress. We cannot take more than one step at a time.

–Orison Swett Marden

Often, the long-term objectives or goals we have for our children seem so broad and far away that it's difficult to connect our day-to-day grind with the adults we're trying to create. Yet each day's effort is a stepping-stone on an obstacle-laden path leading to the adult of tomorrow.

Trouble presents itself in many forms. External obstacles are the easiest to spot from a distance, giving you a bit more time to prepare. These can be starting school or a new grade or moving the family home. The trickier ones are internal because you can't always spot them coming; they pop out of nowhere. These include the almost daily shifting of your child's friendships, his feelings about self, peer pressures, changing hormones and his awakening to independence. These obstacles practically sneak up on you. Acting with focus and purpose during a sneak attack is only possible when you have a firm picture of your objectives planted in your mind. This clear understanding of your true objectives helps you to navigate when the clouds are thick. When your objectives aren't clearly defined, you run the risk of veering terribly off course.

> *A genius is one who shoots at something no one else can see, and hits it.* —Unknown

There is a great deal of stress traveling through a cloud storm. First, you experience confidence-robbing indecision that gets in the way of deliberate action. You start reacting to situations rather than initiating action in alignment with your long-term objectives. Doubt during cloudy times makes a rough ride even more stressful.

After you emerge from the cloud bank, frustration hits you squarely in the face because now you can see just how far off course you've traveled.

To get back on track will take twice as much work and twice the time; it might even mean doubling back altogether to start over. Ouch! So much lost time and extra work that simply being clear in your focus at the start would have prevented.

PEACE FOR TODAY AND PEACE FOR A LIFETIME

Short- and long-term objectives can actually be the same. By this I mean that, by understanding them both, it's possible to structure an action plan that makes them both possible at the same time. Regardless of your goals, taking action using the Peacemaker Parent approach replaces indecision and frustration with purpose and calm during even the cloudiest time so that you can handle obstacles with confidence about the future. Just knowing that you have a great plan that includes the present and the future reduces self-doubt. This is the peace I promise for today. As your kids begin to respond by doing their morning tasks without your involvement, another layer of peace is created. The layers continue to build: confidence and trust layering on top of peace and harmony. Your child will steadily grow into the independent, responsible and self-assured adult you intended all along. This is the peace you're promised for a lifetime.

HOW TO SET OBJECTIVES

You've probably heard some of this goal-setting advice before. Either you've read a thing or two or you've talked to others; but since you're reading this book, I'm guessing you didn't get clear directions on how exactly to do it. It's easy to tell someone to set objectives, and that's why so many people can offer the advice. Figuring out the thorny details of how to guide you through setting those objectives in a thoughtful way isn't so easy, and I believe that's why that bit is missing so much of the time.

> The truth is that parents are not really interested in justice. They just want quiet.   –Bill Cosby

I've come up with a simple, three-step exercise from which your most desired long-term objectives will become clear. Each step is a question you ask yourself about you—not your child. Why you? Two reasons: One, it's much easier to examine what we do as adults now than it is to attempt a guess at what we think our kids will do twenty or more years from now.

The second reason is that we tend to idealize perfection in our children, forgetting that they are just as human as we are. Starting with your personal experiences is a straightforward way to begin the process. So ask yourself the following questions:

1. What do I do for myself in the morning?

2. What do I think about when I do these things?

3. What are the core life skills I use to do them successfully?

Think of the first step as defining your body in action, the second as defining your conscious mind in action and the third as defining your unconscious mind in action. The table on the next page gives you a picture of what I came up with when I did this exercise. Mine is only a partial list; there are so many things to be done every morning and some days require different tasks. I'm giving you an example of a few standard chores to get you started with your own list.

QUESTIONS ABOUT YOUR MORNING

STEP ONE	STEP TWO	STEP THREE
Each Night Before Bed	**Each Night Before Bed**	**Each Night Before Bed**
Set the alarm and snooze	Considering the day ahead and the need for a snooze or two	Thinking ahead Knowing self Accountability
Set the coffee pot	Knowing the importance of the first sip right away	Thinking ahead Knowing self
Lay out my clothes	Considering the next day's activities; verifying the clothes I need are in presentable condition (washed and pressed)	Thinking ahead Verifying Respecting self
In the Morning	**In the Morning**	**In the Morning**
Get up within a couple snoozes	It's better to just get up than to feel rushed	Thinking ahead Accountability Knowing self
Brush my teeth	Wanting a bright smile, fresh breath and healthy teeth	Thinking ahead Respecting self Respecting others Accountability
Make breakfast	Needing to fuel-up well to be productive and happy until lunch	Thinking ahead Knowing self Respecting self Accountability
Make my bed	Organizing my environment keeps me focused and maintains a peaceful home	Thinking ahead Knowing self Respecting others
Leave the house on time	Back into departure time, considering traffic and the need to feel relaxed and be on time	Thinking ahead Knowing self Accountability

Step One

For step one, "what you do," keep it simple. Just think about one day or one week. Make a list; really write a list of the things you have to do. Don't dig too deeply; keep it very simple by focusing only on the actions you take in your daily life that are routine. Step one is pretty easy. (Hint: Everything in life is easy when you take it one step at a time!)

In step two, the "conscious mind in action," ask yourself what you needed to think about in order to do the things on your list well. Did you have to consider other family members or people outside your family? Was it an action to set up another action for later in the day, next week, next year, etc.?

For the final step, the "unconscious mind in action," open your mind to the significance of your overall thought process. These are the most basic themes of your thinking. Was it thinking ahead? Was it having compassion for others? Was it having a deep understanding of your own happiness? Did you feel responsible?

Your lists may be different, and obviously there are a great number of other things we all do, but it doesn't take many specific chores to highlight a pattern. If you think about what you do and then what you need to think about to do it, you are able to see the life skill you used to make it all happen. Notice how thinking ahead and knowing self were core skills used for almost everything? That's no coincidence. The ability to think ahead and understand how you internally process your environment is key to functioning at even basic levels of adulthood. These are good objectives for your children, good targets for which to aim. The trick is getting these skills embedded in the often crowded and chaotic mind of your child. Once you've done the exercise, there is another issue to consider: ripples.

Ripples

If we are to better the future, we must disturb the present.

–Catherine Booth

There is a universal natural law of cause and effect. Everything has a cause and everything has an effect. Everything is connected and it all counts. I use the analogy of ripples on a pond because it creates a great image of the far-reaching effects one simple action has on life as a whole.

In setting the scene, imagine a vast pond whose opposite shore is just barely within sight. You are standing at the water's edge holding a stone in your hand. The stone represents a choice of action. To understand the analogy, I'll plug in a morning scenario using my ten-year-old son Jack before we started using this program. Before I wake Jack, I choose my objective:

- Out the door as usual, reminders (a.k.a. nagging)

- Out the door without nagging

"Out the door as usual" means that I'll need to keep Jack on track by reminding him to make his bed, to get dressed, to brush his teeth, reminding him again to make his bed, reminding him to eat breakfast, reminding him again to get

> *Happiness is not a reward—it is a consequence. Suffering is not a punishment—it is a result.*
> *—Robert Green Ingersoll*

dressed, etc.—you get the picture. "Out the door without nagging" means I don't do the reminding. I'm going to opt for the no-nag morning. Now I have to pick the course of action or the stone I'll throw.

- No nagging / I'm responsible

- No nagging / Jack is responsible

If I'm responsible it means that I'll do many of the tasks for Jack in return for not nagging him to do them. The other option is to let Jack take care of Jack. This isn't as drastic as it might sound because the things that I ask Jack to do in the morning are the same things he has been asked to do every morning for years. Our morning list changes very little: make bed, get dressed, pajamas away, brush (teeth & hair), eat breakfast and ready the backpack. Not heady stuff, and all things practiced over and over. I choose to let Jack be responsible and I wake him, telling him to meet me at the door at 8:30 with all his regular tasks completed. I even hand him a list of the things he needs to do and set a timer so he will know when he needs to be ready to go. He happily agrees and we both move into the morning.

Splash goes the stone in the pond! I'm rewarded with a nag-free morning, and the initial ripples expanding from the splash site are great. I've had time to really prepare myself for the day ahead. I've eaten breakfast, answered a few e-mails and even caught a bit of my favorite morning news program. At 8:30 the timer goes off and Jack slides up to meet me at the door. Here the second ring of ripples begins to surface. Jack arrives dressed as Stupendous Man—black Batman hood, cape and armbands. He hasn't eaten the breakfast laid out and doesn't have any materials needed for school. The house is a wreck—Stupendous Man has more energy than any creature on the planet—and he has bad breath because he didn't brush his teeth. Quite possibly his twelve-year old brother, Michael, is in a similar state because Jack is so distracting when he's Stupendous Man. All of this resulted from my choice of action.

Given the state of my children at the door I now must take more action. I'll either fix the most obvious problems (i.e., clothes, backpacks and breakfast) or let both boys go as they are. I decide to put some pants on Jack and take the boys to school. I'll face a messy house when I get home and I'll probably have extra-hungry mouths to feed at dinner, but I've decided that's okay because I'm just so sick and tired of nagging. Even this isn't too bad—unless, of course, you consider the effects (the ripples) surrounding Jack.

Everything resulting from my choice of action that happens to Jack is at school. Diagram One represents only one ripple: his missing homework. Notice how the rings get bigger as they expand. This represents the way one action grows to have a much greater influence on life as a whole. It's obvious the farther out the ripples expand that being unprepared can become a bigger issue than simply forgetting homework assignments. This is a key part of the analogy when thinking about short-term versus long-term goals. I'm not suggesting that forgetting a fourth-grade assignment will result in a high school dropout living on welfare, but I am suggesting that, over time, your short-term actions create your long-term outcome, whether you are aware of the connection at the time you act or not.

There's another aspect to my diagram, however. The picture presented is of only a few ripples affecting the present and near future. For example, the effects of not having

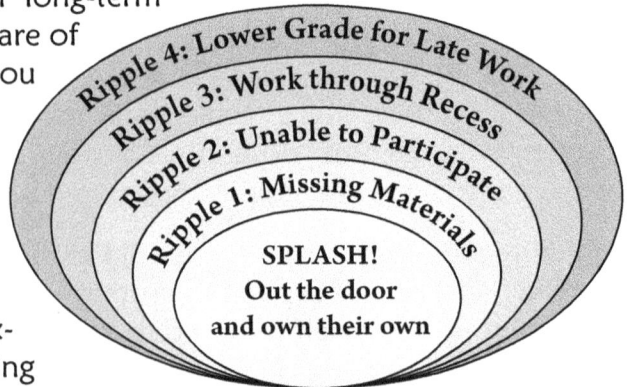

Ripple 4: Lower Grade for Late Work

Ripple 3: Work through Recess

Ripple 2: Unable to Participate

Ripple 1: Missing Materials

SPLASH!
Out the door
and own their own

your homework are: not being able to participate in the classroom project, missing recess to make up the work and receiving a lower grade for it. I purposely illustrated visually in this way because most of us think in the short-term, where the ripples are easy to see and the effects aren't too dire. In reality, the ripples expand well beyond what we can easily see from the shoreline and they continue to grow in size and importance all the way to the other side.

At a certain point, and not too far away at that, we lose track of how specific actions today cause our tomorrow. On this particular morning, for example, I couldn't keep a firm picture in my mind of the objectives I wanted to create because they weren't "close" enough to me. That's when I decided to change my location in the pond, so to speak. Now, I imagine I'm standing in the middle of a pond divided in three sections. The wedge in front of me represents my short-term goals. Tying in the exercise you did earlier, the results of step one go in this forward-facing wedge—your body in action. The wedges to either side are the thoughts and strategies I'll use to accomplish my goals. The side wedges of the pond contain the results from step two—your conscious mind in action. The wedge behind me contains my long-term objectives. Here are the bigger ripples I want to create, that would have expanded beyond my sight if I were still standing on shore. By creating a different mental image I bring the long-away objectives closer, where I can be in touch with them. This back wedge is where you put the results from step three—your unconscious mind in action. Notice how much easier it is to see the connections between goals.

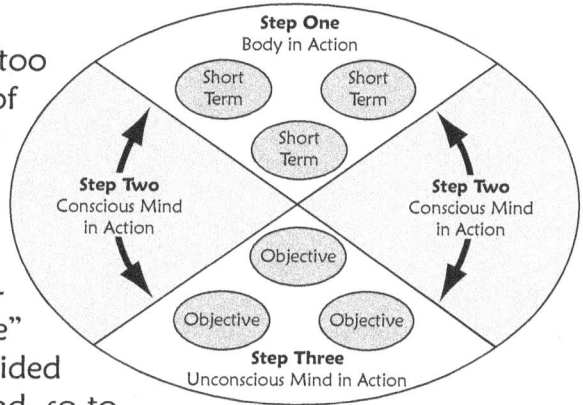

One of my objectives for Jack is accountability. Sending Stupendous Man off to school unprepared, as in the example, won't connect him there. So let's go back to the beginning of this scenario, choose differently and trace the ripples.

REWIND

I stick with the no-nag morning but decide to accept responsibility for Jack being ready and prepared on time by doing many of his chores for him.

Splash! I'm rewarded with an earlier wake-up call so that I'll have time for all the extra work I'll do for Jack. As Jack takes his time getting out of bed, I lay his clothes out and pick up yesterday's clothes off the floor. I go over his school schedule, gathering everything he'll need for the day's activity—such as his trumpet and music book, library books to be returned, the tennis ball he likes to play with at recess, homework done last night and the family-tree poster that's due today. I go back to his room where he is now sitting on the floor in his pajamas, eyeing his Stupendous Man costume. I help him dress by pulling off his pajama top and putting his school shirt on over his head. This continues until both socks are on. He walks out of his room; I make his bed and put away his pajamas. I coax him to breakfast and sit with him to prevent an imaginary adventure from distracting him from eating.

After I clear the dishes, I lead him to the bathroom for teeth brushing, where I've already put the toothpaste on the toothbrush, and I brush his hair. Then it's back downstairs for shoes that I tie and a jacket that I zip. It's 8:30. I hand him his trumpet and backpack, and we're ready to go.

I'm sure that more than a few of you have done all this, and perhaps more, in an attempt to relieve your life of nagging. You're trying to prevent thin-lip wrinkles and that horrible wrinkle between your eyes as you purse and scowl. It seems the only way to stop your shrill, shrieking voice is to just do it yourself. At one point or another you've cried "Uncle!" and given up banging your head against the wall. You realize that no one will ever give you that nickel for every time you've reminded him to put his pajamas away. True, there isn't a fortune in nickels waiting for you; but believe me, there is a simple and peaceful way to get out of the house in the morning without nagging or doing everything yourself. First, let's look at the ripples of this scenario.

> *I'm going to stop punishing my children by saying, "Never mind, I'll do it myself." –Erma Bombeck*

Frustration, worry and stress hit fast. I'm frustrated that I need to be involved to such a degree for Jack to do simple and routine things. I'm worried that he won't ever be able to function successfully without me. I'm also stressed that I'll be late getting myself ready or that I'll forget something critical.

Life is great for Jack. He's fed, happy and prepared for a great day at school. But those are only the ripples you can see close up. What about the effects that spread farther out into the future? Instead of connecting with objectives like independence, responsibility and knowing self, they connect with dependence, irresponsibility and confusion about self. So what do you do?

Being a visual thinker, my new picture of the pond that connects short-term goals and long-term objectives works to keep me headed in the right direction. Whenever I'm in doubt as to how I should act or when I become frustrated

> *Most children threaten at times to run away from home. This is the only thing that keeps some parents going.*   *–Phyllis Diller*

with the short-term results, I simply turn around and look again at my objectives. By tracing the lines from back to front I am always shown the right short-term action to take. So try turning around when you set your objectives or hit a snag.

WHAT IF YOU MISS?

There are just two more things to talk about before we move on. First, what happens when you "miss"? Let's say you do all that I've asked you to do by setting a great objective of independence and high self-esteem. You turn around and check in with your long-term objectives and decide to teach your son to tie his shoes. Off you go, but he doesn't learn to tie his shoes. You think you "missed" because you didn't see the splash you expected—he can't tie his shoes. What do you do when well-thought-out action doesn't work? Most of us try redoubling our efforts by trying several different methods in a sort of shotgun approach. Another is to give up and opt for Velcro. Both those scenarios bring a whole host of effects that confuse your original intent and delay your results. To be sure you stay on track with the original objectives of independence and self-esteem, you will need to check your actions with the back wedge of the pond. If you judge success by short-term results alone, it can look like you missed your mark. The truth is, we always hit what we aim for. It's just that we aren't always looking for the right indicators of success. Keep close touch with your long-term objectives so that you can see the success in what, at first, might seem to be a failure.

There is another option some frustrated parents try. They begin pushing harder, trying to muscle their way through the problem, often going too fast or using negative measures (like ridicule) to get the job done. These actions might lead him back to independence eventually, but they won't ever lead him to high self-esteem.

EXPECTATIONS

*You must have long-range goals to keep you from being
frustrated by short-term failures.*

–Charles C. Noble

Proper expectations are critical to your interpretation of success and peace. Teaching your child to tie shoes will most likely take time, and though it might appear that you "missed" when they attempt and fail repeatedly, you didn't. Taught in a positive, patient and loving manner, tying shoes really is connected to independence and high self-esteem. Staying connected to your objectives will help you stay rightly focused as you teach. With the right expectations you will see the success right away because a tied shoe is only a detail. The excitement your child has when you begin to teach and he begins to learn is the splash you want to see. It's just a matter of time before the shoe-tying skill clicks. In all of this, your proper expectation relieves you of doubt and fills you with a sense of peace and purpose.

A DEER IN THE HEADLIGHTS

It might seem overwhelming to think that everything said or done had to be carefully weighed and considered. Yikes! How would anything get done? If everything we tried to teach needed to be laboriously weighed and measured, it would put us all in therapy! Not to worry: There is a very simple way to hold your objectives calmly in your mind. Notice the life skills you figured out in the earlier exercise. The number of different skills is pretty small in relation to the number of actions we take every day. These skills are the foundation that supports everything else. Think of these as your "core" skills that are at the center of your actions. An apple's core is pretty small in comparison to the apple as a whole, and so is the Earth's core in comparison to the whole planet. So, too, is the number of core skills you need to be happy and successful. This makes keeping track of them easier; and, with practice, your need to turn around and look at them becomes less and less. So don't stress-out. Just make a plan for the end game and then play that game every day to win.

> *True happiness is ... to enjoy the present, without anxious dependence upon the future. –Seneca*

 CHAPTER FOUR

Thinking It Through In Advance

Dig the well before you are thirsty.

–Chinese Proverb

Once you've locked your focus on your objectives, the next step is to develop your peace plan. Paramount to your plan is to ensure all actions connect to both the short- and long-term objectives. There are four areas of action:

1. *Tasks:* The morning chores for which your child will be responsible

2. *Time:* The start and stop parameters for the morning

3. *Incentives:* The reasonable offerings of things (yes, including money) to encourage and reward your child's willing cooperation and efforts

4. *Communication:* The regular meetings you will have with your child to establish the program and review progress

Perhaps the most obvious thing, and the one on which you are most focused right now, is the task list—the list of all the things you want your child to do on his own every morning. The task list might seem like the most important (and

You can't build a reputation on wht you're going to do.

–Henry Ford

perhaps the most difficult) aspect of the morning, but in reality the opposite is true. The particular chores your child attempts to do each morning are only small examples of the larger lessons you're trying to teach. Making a bed without your involvement is just an example of being responsible; the task itself isn't the lesson. That's not to say that the chore is unimportant; but with the Peacemaker approach our focus is trained further into the future, so really any chore can teach the larger lessons for which we are aiming. Viewed in this way it should be easier to put your list together.

If you've tried in the past to teach your child to be responsible it was probably with a heavy focus on the short-term results of his daily tasks. As each one of those past methods failed to work, you probably grew skeptical about *anything* working. The greater the number of failed attempts (that shotgun approach again), the more likely you and your child will be to quickly dismiss another new approach if you don't see the short-term results you expect. It becomes a habit to look for the signs of another failure rather than the (sometimes small) signs of real success. Changing your view from near to far should re-energize and re-prioritize your goals. Thinking it through in advance this time is different, but you still have to guard against skepticism.

With the Peacemaker Parent method applied through the Morning Peacemaker, all actions that you plan for yourself and your child must make clear connections to your long-term objectives. Perhaps this one change will be the difference between seeing the encouraging signs of success and seeing more of the same old disappointment. Ensuring a clear connection between actions and goals keeps you consciously connected to your objectives by reinforcing the *why* of everything you do and expect. Keeping your resolve strong in this way will help you to stay focused if the skepticism tries to creep back in. Another important reason for only including actions that clearly connect to your objective is to ensure that nothing unnecessary or self-defeating is put into play.

SABOTAGE

Self-defeating? Why would anyone include self-defeating or unnecessary actions in her plan? Silly as it may sound, if you include an unnecessary action in your plan, you become a saboteur in disguise. Your current unacceptable situation is the result of your past actions that may have left you with a sour attitude. Though the conscious mind is hungry for peace and resolution, the unconscious mind can interfere by setting up circumstances in which we are actually exacting revenge or avoiding responsibility. Have you ever felt a small sense of relief when you've tried a new approach to something and it didn't work? I have. Maybe you, like I, have at one time or another found relief in a failure because it meant that you didn't have to actu-

> *Advertising may be described as the science of arresting human intelligence long enough to get money from it.*
> *–Stephen Leacock*

ally make changes, or because it somehow proved that change is impossible. There can be consolation in sitting back and thinking that, because you *tried* to solve the problem, you are absolved of the responsibility for not having actually solved it: "I'm trying everything and nothing works." The two big ways in which parents sabotage their success is by buying into the marketing of low-effort methods (like sticker charts) and by creating plans that are too complex to follow.

Hocus Pocus

Many parents want to believe that a generic sticker chart will, all by its self, have magical powers to motivate their children for immediate and long-term success. Even though they know it can't be true, they go along because they simply don't know what is involved or even where to start. They imagine the job will require an enormous amount of effort, or hopefully (abracadabra) magic. Desperately they buy into the marketing scheme that claims great results in children with little effort by their parents. They see pictures of happy children and read testimonials from relieved parents who claim near overnight success once they posted the chart. Wanting to avoid facing what they believe would otherwise be an overwhelmingly difficult feat, they hang their hopes on a chart. When the chart inevitably fails to give them the same magical results about which they read, it's pronounced a complete failure. The failure only deepens their belief that achieving results is really impossible and that further attempts are futile.

All or Nothing

The other saboteur is the parent who plans with too much complexity, having a get-it-all-in-from-the-start attitude. Parents excessively burden everyone when they try to pre-plan every task, every measure of performance, every reward and every contingency. First, it's just plain impossible to have a plan ready ahead of time for every detail un-

> *Too much attention is given to the 'what ifs.'*

less, of course, your plan is to respond to situations as they arise. But when you focus on all the "what ifs," you're most likely creating a swirling funnel of negative fault-finding energy.

There are two kinds of "what ifs": the "what if he does" and the "what if he doesn't." The over-planning parent probably spends most of her time preparing excessively for the "doesn't." She becomes consumed with creating a box around each task so that the child cannot possibly avoid giving anything but perfection. This parent plans every detail to prevent her child from taking advantage of a loophole. By concentrating on what the child might not do or might try to avoid, this nearsighted parent sabotages the child's learning process. Besides, whose responsibility is it to get the bed made anyway? I mean, if you believe it is your responsibility to have planned for everything, you must also believe that anything less than your expected result is due to your faulty planning, right? Wouldn't that make the short-term outcome your responsibility? Maybe yes and maybe no; but at the very least the lines of responsibility are blurred. It might make such a parent add even more to her already complex plan. The over-planned approach will fail because it is unreasonable to have planned for every what-if, just as it is unreasonable to expect radical changes in short-term results to happen all at once.

KISS It (Keep It So Simple)

Simplicity is the secret to creating a plan that squarely places the responsibility with the child while demonstrating your trust and confidence in him. A simple plan is easy to remember and can be consistently followed. Your child will relax and feel free to experiment with responsibility, knowing from the start that any failure in the short-term is just an expected part of the learning process.

When either the low-effort parent or the overly-complicated planner walks away from a failed attempt, each feels equally justified that she has done all she could and nothing worked. She allows herself to think that forces beyond her control are at work and, therefore, she is absolved from the responsibility for not getting the results she wanted. But just like your child, you are accountable; your child still needs to learn to be responsible and you still need a peaceful home. This time, however, rather than finding a reason to justify giving up, thinking like a Peacemaker Parent will enable you to succeed.

Can't I Just Take a Pill or Something?

For more than twenty years I have been a professional fitness coach and I have seen over and over again how clients sabotage themselves in much the same way as the parents I just described. There are those who train with little effort and others who have the do-it-all-now approach. The low-effort clients book sessions but have reason after reason for cancelling them. The appointments they keep consistently start late and are filled with more "good" reasons why they can't perform fully. They talk and talk and talk to avoid training because, down deep, they don't believe it will work anyway. Many of these clients bought into the marketing hype of fad diets, diet pills and magical gadgets that practically do the exercising for them! Of course, these tools failed; there are no quick fixes here, just like there are no magical sticker charts. But they wanted to believe the promise that a low-effort method would give them immediate success, so they hoped and tried and failed. These clients are frustrated now and don't believe that the changes they want are actually possible for them. Rather than try again, they just go through the motions with little effort so they can feel absolved of their responsibility for not succeeding—"I'm trying everything and I still can't lose any weight." They want to convince themselves and everyone around them that, as long as they look like they are trying and have really good reasons for failure, not losing thirty pounds is just as good as having lost thirty pounds.

Other clients want to change everything at once: eliminate all fat, sugar, carbohydrates and alcohol from their diets while training rigorously right from the start. Ok—while there are people out there who have the discipline to make such radical changes in their diet and exercise program all at once, the majority of us can't. In fact, if you have thirty pounds to lose, chances are good that those thirty pounds are the result of

> *The ability to simplify means to eliminate the unnecessary so that the necessary may speak.*
> *–Hans Hoffman*

your past inability to set limits and follow through with other fitness plans. These clients come to me with complex plans expecting one or two training sessions each week to magically infuse them with the willpower to sustain the radical changes they've planned. The level of effort and discipline needed to meet their action plans consistently are unreasonable and will be pronounced a failure when they don't lose 30 pounds in two weeks. They begin with an all-or-nothing expectation—hoping for all, but quick to accept nothing.

Both of these clients want better lives, but neither unconsciously believes she will ever have it; so both sabotage their efforts without really being aware of it. They are either unwilling or unable to see greater potential success in small initial changes, so they find reasons to give up. It bears repeating that getting the results you want—losing those thirty pounds or having a nag-free morning and responsible children—is *not* the same as not getting those results but having really good reasons why.

CONNECT THE DOTS

For you to achieve the objectives you have for your child you must start small and keep it so simple. Let's use the milestones of learning to ride a bicycle as an example. You planned a gradual progression of tricycles to training wheels that eventually led to two-wheeled bicycles. You didn't start them out on a complicated bike with gears and hand brakes; wisely, you made their first bicycle low to the ground and simple to operate. It made sense to start small there just as it makes perfect sense to start small here too. Connect all actions in the morning to your objectives. By drawing a line between them you will develop an understanding of the true amount of effort needed to accomplish your goal—and it prevents you from planning unnecessary actions.

> *About all the average person learns from his mistakes is how to be an expert at making excuses.*
> *–Unknown*

Figure 1 illustrates over-planning in making a bed. Remember, making the bed is but one example of the achievement of the real objective of being responsible. So if you plan several actions for one task, you're adding too many gadgets to that first bicycle and a red flag should pop up telling you that you're getting off track.

Stop and think about each action surrounding the task of making a bed and eliminate the following types of actions:

- Actions that are overly complicated for the child to perform

- Actions requiring your assistance or approval

- Actions that you are unwilling or unable to support consistently

DO FIRST

All 4 decorative pillows
at head of bed

Pull bed away from wall
to tuck in comforter

**MAKE
BED**

Get Mom to check
when done

Comforter is smooth
and hangs straight

Sheets flat under
comforter

All 10 stuffed animals
in line by pillows

Figure 1

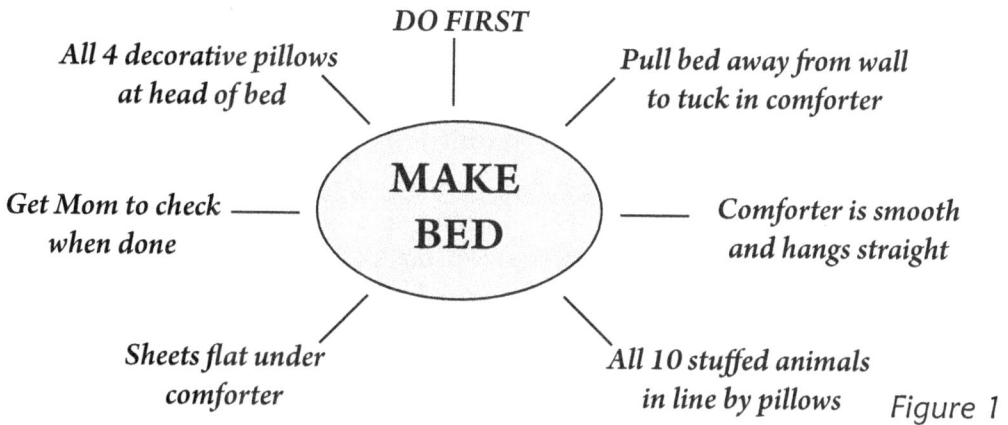

Figure 2 illustrates the same task with a much more manageable set of actions planned.

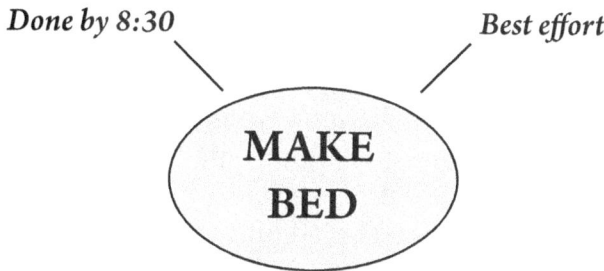

Done by 8:30

Best effort

**MAKE
BED**

Figure 2

You can quickly see the benefit of simplicity. Your child will relax and be encouraged to try. To approach his bed each day dreading an overly compli-cated standard he doesn't believe he can achieve will overwhelm him and paralyze his actions. Give your child the freedom to do his best and he will be empowered to find a way that works for his body and his skill level. As you support the child's efforts you support the long-term objectives. He will still need your help occasionally but, without fear of judgment, your child will come to you and ask for it rather than give up and blame you. When this happens see it as a huge victory! Asking for help is the first sign that your child trusts your support and feels responsible for finding strategies to get the job done. Hurray! Your plan is working!

> *Don't be more precise than the subject warrants.* –Plato

When I discuss this scenario with parents many are reluctant to relax quality standards and allow their children to give only a "best effort." They want to teach their children the importance of doing a good job and they are afraid the freedom to do their "best" gives the children a license to do a half job with full reward. First, you must keep reminding yourself that the bed isn't really the objective. Second, while I agree that a job well done is critical, the true meaning of a job well done is that it is the best job you can do. Allow for your children's differing sizes, abilities and maturity levels in deciding what you will accept as their best efforts. There are many little things that, as adults, we take for granted because of our size and experience. It's not easy for a five-year-old to figure out how to pull up sheets and make the blanket straight when he can't reach over the bed. With short arms and bodies they simply can't do it the same way we can. The child needs to experiment with different approaches to get the job done, such as kneeling at the top of the bed to pull the sheets up and then working out how to get off the bed again without messing up the whole thing. Lining up ten animals and four pillows, as in Figure 1, requires an attention to detail that the child might not yet possess. I tell parents that, if a perfectly made bed is critical to them, their choices are to either simplify the process for the child or to continue making the bed themselves.

> *Never tell people how to do things. Tell them what to do and they will surprise you with their ingenuity.*
> *–General George Patton*

Simplifying the bed may mean that only one special stuffed animal stays on the bed while the others come off and "live" on a chair next to the bed. It may mean the four decorative pillows and even the top sheet aren't used for a while so the child has only one pillow and a blanket to deal with. Maybe the bed is repositioned in the room so that the child can access both sides easily. The point is that, by continuing to draw connecting lines from actions to objectives, you reinforce the need for simplicity; a picture-perfect bed isn't needed for responsibility to be learned.

What's Left Is Fear

Don't worry about the world coming to an end today. It is already tomorrow in Australia.

–Charles M. Schulz

I find that after all the superficial excuses for not achieving the results parents want are put aside the one emotion fueling it all is usually fear: fear of being taken advantage of, fear of appearing weak to their children or other adults, and fear that they will mess it up. The bottom line is that they are afraid they can't teach their children how to accomplish the worthy goals they set for them.

If that is the way you think, it must change; but it can only change slowly, so relax. The programming you've operated with up until now has taken years to develop and is rooted deep in your unconscious. Changing it will take time, but it really isn't that difficult if you relax.

There is an analogy that I learned from James Arthur Ray in his book *The Science of Success*, which beautifully illustrates the process of change. Think about a glass of cranberry juice as your current thinking and your new thinking as clear water. To fill your glass with the water you might think it fastest to simply empty out the cranberry juice and re-fill the glass with the water. That's the all-at-once thinking that just doesn't work. The only real sustainable way to make changes to your thinking is to go slowly. Start by adding the water to the glass of juice. As you pour in the water the cranberry juice starts to overflow out of the glass. The juice is being diluted—changed— even before you actually see the physical signs. If you keep pouring the water you will keep pushing out the old cranberry juice until, one day, only clear water will be in the glass. This is just how your thinking will begin to change as you reinforce your objectives by connecting actions to them.

Changing your existing beliefs will take some time. It's very important that, as you go through planning actions, you realize your need to progress slowly, too. You and your children started out together with clearly defined roles; you provided everything and they relied on you totally. This relationship worked well for years until it was time for them to learn to do a few things on their own. As they learned to use the toilet and to drink from a cup on their own, your relationship began to change.

> *Fear is the thought of admitted inferiority.*
> –Elbert Hubbard

It started out easily because your child responded in ways you expected and you had the right tools to help bridge the gap between their dependence on you for these things and their independence. The tools you used helped you both ease slowly into the new independent relationship. You could relax knowing the pull-up diapers and lidded sippy cups were there when accidents happened. Gradually letting go felt safe and natural for you both.

> *A jug fills drop by drop.*
> *–Buddha*

The transition took time. If you consider the scenario of teaching your child to drink from a cup without the right tools, how frustrating and difficult the experience would have been. Instead of beginning the process when he was one or two years old, you might have waited until he was three, four or even older. But you were able to start the process earlier because there were tools that gradually progressed (successively progressed) his independence at the same pace as his increasing physical and mental abilities.

We can clearly see the child's progression as he moved from baby bottles that you held for him, to bottles with handles, to lidded plastic cups and so on. What you may not have recognized, however, was the progression in you: the letting go (both physically and emotionally) as you gradually moved back to let your child become independent. As you went from holding the bottle to allowing him to hold his own bottle, you were still ready to help when he needed it. As your confidence in his increasing skills grew, your ability to let go also grew. It would be so much more difficult to decide it was time he was on his own and force a restriction on yourself to not pick up his bottle when it fell. Turning off your deeply rooted programming to respond to his needs isn't like flipping a switch. I think it would be an unreasonable expectation and it would feel so wrong. You needed the time and the practice to let go, just as much as he needed time and practice to be ready for you to let go.

The same applies to his learning how to be responsible and independent except that, until now, there were no tools, no sippy cups or training wheels to rely on during the transition. So when the urge to get-it-all-in up-front arises, stop a minute and remember that you are also learning something—learning to let go. And with the Morning Peacemaker tools to support you both, it will feel gradual and natural.

PRACTICE MAKES PERFECT

> *Find victories in attempts,*
> *not defeat in failures.*

Be easy on yourself and your child by keeping everything simple. If you want your child to make his bed, show him how you might approach the job, practice with him and then let him do it his way without interference for a while. Let him make it messy and wrong at first. The objective isn't to teach him to make his bed according to a strict standard, but rather to teach him to be responsible for this morning chore. Keep reminding yourself about the objective so that, when you walk by his room and the bed isn't made very well at first, you see a successful attempt at responsibility and not a failed attempt at making a bed.

Let's Get This Party Started: The Task List

Satisfaction lies in the effort, not in the attainment.
Full effort is full victory.

–Mahatma Gandhi

Ok, now it's time to draft a soft outline for the morning. I use the word "soft" because it is critical to the success of this program that you allow room for your child's input. You must reserve a large portion of ownership for him. Your outline is simply the starting point for discussion. The actual list only becomes a working plan when your child has contributed and everyone agrees. In drafting your outline, ask yourself the following questions:

- What are the morning tasks I want him to do?

  - What will he think he should do?

  - Are any tasks, such as bathing, not consistently needed each day?

  - Are any tasks, like homework, critical?

  - Are any tasks, such as taking medication, mandatory for the morning?

- Which tasks do I think he currently performs well?

  - Which tasks will he think he currently performs well?

  - What is it about these tasks that make them easy?

- Which tasks do I help with now?

  - Which tasks will he think I help him with?

  - Is help asked for or do I just step in?

  - Do I argue with him over any of these tasks?

– What is it about the task that makes it difficult?

– How can the task be simplified?

• How long should each of the tasks take?

– How long do they usually take now?

– How long will he think it takes to do each one?

When developing your outline, first think about the morning and all the tasks from your perspective and then see them from your child's perspective. It's important that you understand why you feel each task is necessary so you are ready to support it with more than "Because I said so." I'm not suggesting you prepare for a battle of wills or anticipate a struggle over every task; in fact, you'll probably find the opposite is actually true. But there may be a task that is not readily acceptable to your child—for example, the importance of brushing hair in the morning. I experienced this very issue with my son, Jack. He felt that brushing his hair was only necessary if he were going to a wedding, and certainly not necessary for just going to school. When we discussed the importance of grooming as part of respecting oneself and others, he understood why he needed to do it but still didn't want to do it. Together we found a compromise: a short hairstyle that required very little morning maintenance. Because we were both focused on finding a way to meet the true need for the task, we could compromise and move on. At the time, Jack was eight and not concerned about his appearance. Now, at ten, he is a bit more style conscious and chooses to wears his hair longer. His decision to grow his hair included prior consideration for his need to brush it in the morning. He knew he would be accountable for his grooming and accepted the responsibility willingly because he wanted the longer style. Score! Be open, and you will score, too.

> *The man who moves a mountain begins by carrying away small stones. –Confucius*

SOME DOS AND DON'TS

• DO limit the number of morning tasks to six or seven at first. For younger children, or children with special needs, you may start out with only one or two really simple tasks. As they grow and gain confidence you can add more.

- DON'T include a task that isn't done consistently, such as bathing every other day; consider changing bath time to the night before to keep the morning consistent, especially at first. Once he gets the hang of things you can consider moving it back to the morning.

- DO include a task that signifies the end of the morning's responsibilities, such as checking off each task completed.

- DON'T include any task that cannot be done at another time of day, such as taking medication. When he begins the tasks on the list he must be free to try and fail without harmful consequences. For example, if your child forgets to brush his teeth in the morning, he can simply brush them later in the day. Stinky breath is the only real consequence to learning.

- DON'T include a task that your child is not mature enough to complete on his own, such as homework. In my house homework often requires my assistance and the re-direction of my sons' focus. Since it isn't optional to do or not to do homework, it must be completed the night before to prevent my need to assist and/or redirect actions in the morning.

ARE WE THERE YET? HOW MUCH TIME DO I HAVE?

Time's fun when you're having flies.

–Kermit the Frog

It's best to back into the time parameters for the morning. Think about how much time is needed for each task, and consider the time you leave the house. Then back into the best time for wake-up and for tasks to begin. Be sure to allow double or triple the time for each task if possible so that the pressure is off. Let's say your child is old enough to brush his teeth without your supervision. The dentist recommends a full two minutes of actual brushing. Even if your child spends that amount of time brushing (most kids don't—at least not on a consistent basis), avoid allowing only two minutes for this task. There can be a whole lot of important daydreaming and role-playing in front of a bathroom mirror, so make sure you allow time for it. Instead

Allow time for role-playing and daydreaming. Preset timers will bring them back to task automatically.

of two minutes you might allow ten. Each morning task should be viewed in just this way until you come to reasonable time parameters.

Also, consider your child's body rhythm. Is he a slow starter in the morning or does he jump out of bed and hit the ground running? One note of caution: In your attempt to allow ample time, avoid allowing too much. If the time parameters are spread too far apart your child won't feel how even the smallest distraction affects the morning routine. Along with all the other lessons, make sure your child is practicing time management, too. My children and I agreed that one hour is plenty of time for the following tasks:

- Make bed

- PJs away

- Get dressed

- Brush hair & teeth

- Eat breakfast

- Pack backpack

- Calendar page

Notice that things like homework, bathing and cleaning their rooms are not on the morning list. Even though they are now twelve and ten years old and have been practicing being responsible in the morning for nearly two years, they still aren't ready for responsibilities of greater impact at that time of day. I also avoided including the task of tidying their rooms before school because it would require me to determine acceptability or set a number of guidelines. I decided that I could live with a bed that isn't perfect, but I wasn't ready to allow too much leeway in the overall state of their rooms, so they tidy up before bed. It's actually better this way, since it creates a safe environment for everyone at night. If you've ever stepped on a Lego piece in the dark with bare feet, you know what I mean!

PAY DAY: INCENTIVES

So you think that money is the root of all evil. Have you ever asked what is the root of all money?

–Ayn Rand

Your outline must also include incentives. It is reasonable for any person, no matter how small, to expect something in return for his efforts. That "something" can be anything that lights him up and gets him excited about doing his job. No matter what you offer your children as an incentive, understand that you are paying them for their effort. Does that make you cringe? I know many parents balk at the thought of "paying" their children to do their chores. They expect their children to do their chores automatically as contributing members of the household. "I'm not getting paid to make my bed, why should they get an extra reward for just doing the basics?" I completely understand this sentiment because it comes from the old way of thinking. It focuses on the short-term that has been tainted by past failed attempts to fix things. Some other parents have the attitude, "You'll do it because I told you to do it," and turn away at the thought of offering a reward to their children for doing what they are told to do. Maybe these parents' past efforts included incentives that came to feel like bribes and they are sick and tired of being taken advantage of.

> *If you pay peanuts, you get monkeys.*
> *–James Goldsmith*

I've also met parents who think rewards can be anything except money; that money is the line between incentive and bribe. They are perfectly willing to offer toys or a visit to the zoo but cash is entirely different and, to them, it sends the wrong message. But there is a vast difference between incentives and bribes, and both have definite places in parenting. There is nothing like a good, out-and-out bribe to get your child motivated to do something he really doesn't want to do. We all respond well to bribery. For example, my husband once bribed me to behave during an interview at our country club. As a formality, all new spouses of existing members had to be interviewed by a committee to ensure the spouse was aware of the club's policies and to confirm his/her suitability for membership. Talk about balk! I thought it the most outrageous and condescending thing. I grew up very humbly in the mid-west where country clubs were only for the rich. I had a preconceived notion about the uppity class of people who were about to look down their long, pointed noses at me. My feelings weren't based on fact, because I had had almost no experience with country clubs before; but it didn't make any difference to me. I rejected the idea of being "approved as suitable," though really, I was just afraid I wouldn't know what to say.

On the evening of the interview, I was primed with sarcastic quips and snappy comebacks that would show them that they couldn't intimidate me and they had no right to judge me. Ha! I'd show them. My husband was beside himself. He understood how I felt and where those feelings came from, but he also knew I wouldn't continue to feel that way once I gave the people and the place a chance. Because he didn't want me to create a problem out of a situation that was simply a formality, he bribed me. It wasn't money or jewelry or anything of value; he just offered to take me to my favorite fast-food restaurant right after the interview as a "thank you" for holding back my quips.

I was bribed with Taco Bell!

His gentle bribe did three things for me: It showed me he knew how difficult the situation was for me; It made me laugh and lightened my mood; And it gave me a reason to relax my high-and-mighty attitude without denting my pride. It worked, and I am proud to say that I'm grateful for his willingness to bribe me. Without his intervention I might have said things that could have ruined the possibility of developing some of the friendships I now have. I still cringe at the thought of any panel of people sitting in judgment of another person, but I realize that we are often required to present ourselves to others for jobs or club memberships in order to move forward.

Here is another example of a good use of bribes: Imagine you need your four-year-old son to sit still and be quiet for an hour-and-a-half in church while people he doesn't even know baptize their baby. He must sit on a hard bench in fussy clothes (maybe even a tie!) when all he wants to do is run up and down the aisle sock skating! This is a great time to employ the bribe. It acknowledges his complete unwillingness to cooperate, yet it empowers him to do what you ask without denting his pride. Sitting still under these extreme circumstances, just because you tell him he must, won't motivate him and it might even backfire. But a good old-fashioned bribe will put the situation in a whole new light. The bribe need not be big; it could be as simple as a donut after the service, a quarter or a Hot Wheels car. Regardless of the "thing," it will be seen by him as a really good reason to cooperate.

That is a bribe and a bribe is a beautiful thing when used properly for those kinds of out-of-the-ordinary events.

An incentive, however, is completely different than a bribe. Incentives are standard-and-expected pay for standard-and-expected work. Work is defined as whatever the child sees as work. As adults we may not think it's work to make our bed or brush our teeth, but a child might; and since perception is reality, you must deal with the reality of the child's perception. He doesn't want to get up and make his bed any more than you want to get up and go to work. You go to work, though, because you get paid a regular-and-expected amount for your regular-and-expected job. When you are asked to do more at work, aren't you looking for more incentive? More pay? Of course you are.

> *Reality is merely an illusion, although a very persistent one.*
> —*Albert Einstein*

The same holds true for your children. When they were babies you made their beds and you brushed their teeth; you tidied their toys and packed their things when they went out. As the responsibility for those tasks shifts to them, it will feel like extra work. Why wouldn't they want something extra in return? Your praise for their jobs well done will only satisfy them for so long; at some point they are going to want "stuff." Before they understand what money is all about you can get away with stickers, toys, trips, treats, etc. I encourage that for as long as you can make it work, but be prepared to ante-up when things change.

> *Being young is not having any money; being young is not minding not having any money.* —*Katherine Whitehorn*

There is an infinite number of incentives you can offer your children, ranging from trinkets to planning a family meal, so be open to anything that lights them up, because whatever you offer will only incent them to "work" if they value the incentive. Would you go to work for a sticker? Even a whole book of stickers? That might seem like a silly analogy, but would you go to work for less than what you consider a fair wage, even if your boss said he thought it was fair? Your perception of what is fair is reality for you. Your boss, if she is smart, should try to meet your expectation as incentive for your continued work. You need to do the same for your children.

Do as I Say, Not as I Do

Too often we look at our children as an opportunity to correct all the mistakes we've made. We tell our children stories about the lessons we learned the hard way in order to spare them those kinds of experiences. We want them to avoid wasting time making mistakes, and to eliminate all the behaviors or qualities in themselves that we consider undesirable. If only it worked. Some mistakes are necessary; this is the central theme of the Peacemaker Parent. If you believe that talking to your child about mistakes and goodness will automatically result in a mistake-free and selfless child, you will be disappointed. You will also miss recognizing him as a human being who is perfect in his imperfection. It is not greed, but human nature in action, when your child wants material things. And how else can he get those things but through you?

> *Human beings make mistakes. I know of no supervisory action we can take that will prevent that. I know of no legislation to help us prevent them from making dumb mistakes.*
> *–Alan Greenspan.*

Your child's idea of a reward is in direct proportion to his experiences. When he is young the circle of experience is small in relation to yours; therefore, his idea of reward will seem small to you: a sticker or a scoop of ice cream. But as your child grows and experiences more, the circle expands and, along with that, comes a change in his idea of reward. While he might be satisfied with a sticker for a while, as he is introduced to new things, he will begin to want more. It's normal and expected. When a new model car is released or a new season's fashions hit the magazines or you read about an exciting vacation spot, aren't you moved to want more? Your experiences may have taught you how to balance your new desires with your current circumstances, but you can't expect your child to have that kind of maturity or breadth of knowledge. Both you and your child experience the same emotions regarding wanting more; it's just that he doesn't yet have the same filters.

> *Is the glass half full or half empty? It depends on whether you're pouring or drinking. –Bill Cosby.*

Be realistic when you think incentives through. Wanting "stuff" or money in return for a job isn't always a sign of greed, manipulation or even laziness. While inner pride in a job well done is a huge part of the child's reward, he may still need something more. You and I have the opportunity to choose jobs that can give both inner satisfaction and outward reward, but children are stuck. They can't always choose to do things that give them inner satisfaction so the outward reward can be even more important. The bottom line is, even if you cringe at the thought of offering incentives, you just have to get over it and start thinking like your child.

Be open to paying them, and feel good about it. You can even come up with a barter system, if that works. The point is to incent them to want to try. Whatever you do to reward your children for their efforts will promote them and make them excited to try even harder. You might even discover that they aren't motivated by what you thought, and they might not try their best for money alone. They might really want more time with friends or a special treat in addition to cash. Don't forget that, as adults, we view incentives differently than kids do. Money, for us, means opportunity; but children sometimes don't see it quite

> *Bait the hook with a worm the fish wants.*
> *–Unknown*

that way. Even if they understand the freedom that comes with having their own money, having to save for something big can cause them to lose interest. They want it now, and anything other than now is never. Not a very good incentive. Be open to all these factors and have an idea of what you think they might really desire. Great if it can be stickers, but still great if it's a couple of dollars. Most families try to give an allowance to their children anyway. Teaching the value of money is important and giving the kids a way to earn it is an important part of that lesson. So if you balk at the thought of paying your children to make their beds and brush their teeth in the morning, consider these things:

1. If you give them an allowance without asking for anything in return, you may just be handing them money for nothing.

2. Wanting money is not a sign of a greedy child, but rather a sign of his desire for independence.

3. Learning to be responsible and accountable isn't limited to their morning tasks; the money they earn is something for which they are also responsible and accountable.

Once your mornings are smooth and peaceful you won't even flinch at the thought of giving them incentives. You will want to give to them because you are so happy.

COMMUNICATION

Two monologues do not make a dialogue.

–Abraham Lincoln

Author Anthony J. D'Angelo wrote, "Your mind is like a parachute. It only works if it is open." If there is one thing you must unfailingly do, it is keep your mind open to everything your child says. What he thinks and feels may not always come out well-spoken and succinct. It might wander and meander, it might even sound farfetched, but it must all be considered by you. The fact that your children might not have enough experience to articulate their thoughts and feelings in a way meaningful to you doesn't mean they don't have meaningful thoughts and feelings. Just like everything else, they have to practice communicating their ideas. By being open and positive about everything they say, you will encourage them to say more because they will begin to trust your motives. Value their thoughts and they will value this program. Incorporate their ideas and they will own the program. When they feel ownership, they feel accountable.

Trust must thrive before there can be success. To get to trust you must journey through a few necessary transition points. It's like the children's song that teaches about the body, "The ankle bone is connected to the shin bone, the shin bone is connected to the knee bone..." If you follow the song all the way up you get to the head bone, right? But you can't get to the head bone unless you journey up through all the transition points. If we made a song like that for trust, it would go like this: "Communication is connected to consideration, consideration is connected to compromise, compromise is connected to cooperation and cooperation is connected to trust." It's a road map with only one right path. Watch out for false turns, though, because they lead to dead ends. If you happen to get stuck, just double back and start over because you can definitely get there from here.

MEETINGS

In Chapter Seven, "Finally Meeting Face to Face," you will find the details of how to structure and conduct regular meetings with your child. Review time is an opportunity to help your child with strategies, to nurture the trust that is growing and to pay him. As part of planning your actions, you must think about your willingness and ability to communicate with your child at regular, prearranged times. Just how much time is needed for meetings depends on a few factors:

- The number and ages of your children

- Any special needs your children have

- The number of morning tasks

- The number of past attempts at fixing the morning, i.e., previous sticker charts and other failed attempts

In general, the higher the number in any of these factors, the longer the initial meetings will take. It's best to budget thirty minutes for each meeting during the first month or so. You won't be speaking with your children about issues for thirty minutes, however, because you will be calculating their successful mornings from the previous week and you will be handing out their incentive pay.

Initially there will be some tinkering with the system, too. Even though you will meet with your child prepared with a simple action plan that has completely considered your child's point of view, changes will be made in the beginning until a comfortable and mutually agreeable system for the morning is solidified. For now, keep in mind that regular meetings are critical and you must be prepared to participate consistently.

How often you meet is also important. You must allow enough time between meetings for your child to work with the agreed-upon set of strategies. There are going to be first impressions about things that will change as they practice and learn to overcome obstacles. Meeting too often won't allow them time enough in the saddle to get the feel of the ride. Meeting too infrequently won't allow for necessary tinkering before a task is simply ignored rather than fixed to be functional. Also, too infrequent meetings won't allow the repetition of communication that is necessary for both you and your child to develop a rapport of cooperation and trust.

COOLING OFF PERIOD

Avoid having impromptu meetings mid-week. Emotions and frustrations confuse true thoughts and escalate otherwise small issues into big ones. Limiting discussions to the structure of weekly reviews allows for cooler heads to prevail and real dialogue to happen. My children and I have experienced the benefits of this cooling off period. We've had frustrations hit us mid-week and have wanted to make immediate changes to the working agreement right then and there. At the time of the emotion, it seems perfectly reasonable to make whatever change we think is better than the agreed plan. In the beginning this occurred often, on both sides. I found it difficult to keep my lips zipped when it looked like they were wasting time or rushing through tasks; they found it hard to accept an unsuccessful task without blaming the task or the time allowed. But by the time we came together to talk, the situation that had frustrated us was either completely unimportant or we could discuss it objectively without an accusing tone in anyone's voice.

> *I have noticed that nothing I never said ever did me any harm.*
> *–Calvin Coolidge*

ONE FINAL THOUGHT: COMMITMENT

Endurance is patience concentrated.

–Thomas Carlyle

The final bit of thinking you must do before approaching your child with this program is about your commitment. Though the results you want for the long-term will be achieved with every one of their short-term attempts, it's not always easy to see it that way. It might be tough at times to congratulate your child on his failed attempt to remember to brush his teeth in the morning. Your first thought, at least in the beginning, might be simply that he did not brush his teeth. However, each time he tries, succeeding or failing, your long-term objective is brought closer. His attempt at managing his time and responsibilities is worth congratulating, even if he didn't quite make it all happen. Brushed teeth or not, as long as

> *By prevailing over all obstacles and distractions, one may unfailingly arrive at his chosen goal or destination.*
> *–Christopher Columbus*

you are consistent in your support for his efforts to accomplish his tasks, you are teaching him to be accountable. Remember, too, that any task that isn't completed in the morning is completed later in the day. The teeth will be brushed every day; the only option for your child is to have it count for incentive pay or not. A word of encouragement during a failed attempt is worth more than a whole book of praise after a success. And, as you congratulate his effort, remember to congratulate your own.

The problem is that, initially, it isn't easy to think in this way consistently. When your child arrives at the door, ready to leave for the day without having brushed his teeth, it will be difficult for either of you to see the victory. How not having brushed his teeth is getting him closer to respecting himself and others might be impossible to see, but it is. A child must try and fail with as much support from you as when he tries and succeeds, because failure and success are equal parts of learning. One teaches you what to do and the other teaches what not to do. Each is equally important in understanding how things work. You must continue to remind yourself and your child that this is a learning experience and that a huge part of figuring it all out is looking at each attempt to find what did or did not work. As you remind him of this, you are also reminding yourself. Think of it as win-or-learn, not win-or-lose.

> *Everyone's allowed an occasional failure— except a skydiver, of course.*
> *—Unknown*

The inventor of the light bulb, Thomas Edison, said about his experience inventing the light bulb, "I never failed once. It just happened to be a 2,000-step process." Edison had the commitment to see victory in every attempt, and so must you. I wonder how many other smart men or women had the same idea as Edison but lacked his perspective. When the invention was released I'll bet there were at least a few scientists who kicked themselves for having given up too soon. The only way you can fail to achieve the results you are looking for is to lose the connection to your long-term objectives and give up.

> *Many of life's failures are people who did not realize how close they were to success when they gave up.*
> *—Thomas Edison*

Depending upon the nature of your child, changes may either be easy or difficult, fast or slow. It is a process that is as individual and unique as a fingerprint. Some people are naturally more open to change and others are more hesitant. If you think back to the earlier analogy of the glass of cranberry juice, imagine the size of the opening at the top of the glass as the indicator of your openness to change. The wider the opening on the glass, the easier change will be for you. Some people, like my son Jack and me, have a fairly wide opening at the top of the glass while others, like my husband Ralph and my other son Michael, have more narrow openings. To transition from cranberry juice to water we still have to pour the water into the existing glass of juice, but it's the size of the opening at the top of the glass that dictates the speed at which we can pour. If I pour water from a pitcher into Jack's glass, I can pour water in at a fast pace. If I pour water at the same pace into Michael's glass, most of the water I pour won't even go into the glass because the opening is smaller. I can only make changes to his glass of cranberry juice at the speed dictated by the size of the opening at the top of his glass. Simply said, I can only expect Michael to change according to his ability to accept change.

Being a person who is open to change made understanding the slower pace in Michael's abilities harder to understand. Before I understood his nature, I pushed too hard, poured too quickly and was frustrated with the results. It got very messy and he actually closed up even more. It wasn't until I understood that he was simply responding to change according to his nature, and not consciously thwarting my attempts to teach him, that we both relaxed. It's like having a pushy salesman try to close a deal too hard and fast. Even if you believe the deal he is offering is good, his attempt to make you close faster than you're comfortable with can cause you to be suspicious and you'll want to slow the transaction down. Sometimes, the faster you go, the longer it takes.

If you have children like I do, who are wired in different ways, go at the pace of the one needing the most time. This is not a race to the finish line, because there isn't really a finish line. As a parent, you are on the job for life; so sit back and enjoy the scenery with your child as you both wind through the countryside at a comfortable pace.

CHAPTER FIVE

What We Do For Children

The first half of our lives is ruined by our parents and the second half by our children.

—Clarence Darrow

Have you ever heard the saying, "You've put the cart before the horse?" We hear that from others when we've reversed the necessary order of things. When it comes to the current methods used to teach children accountability and responsibility, the cart is before the horse too, but with a twist. Applying this scenario to our children, we have been skipping the step of empowering their action when we expect them to act. In essence, we have put the child in the cart as we climb onto the horse's back with the reins. It's all fine and dandy until the phone rings and you get down to answer. The horse, a metaphor for action, stops moving. Even if that reward sticker is stuck to the bed the child is supposed to make, the child won't get there with an idle horse. It's maddening to return from your call and find everything exactly as it was. But even if the child said "giddy-up," without the parent goading the horse from behind, that child isn't going anywhere. Without teaching the child how to get the horse moving on his own, we set ourselves up to be needed before he can take action.

So what is the real lesson we teach using these methods? It's not independence, accountability, time management or how to initiate action. Unfortunately, all we are really teaching the child is to be dependent, to blame others (in this case, you, for not being there to guide his actions) and to make excuses. If your child has ever said it was your

"SUING THE FAST FOOD INDUSTRY DIDN'T WORK. I'M STILL FAT!"

fault he didn't have time to make the bed, or blamed you for forgetting his homework, you've experienced this lesson firsthand. The child sitting in the cart was waiting for your reminder, giddy-up horsey; and if, one day, you didn't give the reminder, he felt justified in blaming you for the outcome.

When parents begin using a sticker chart or other program, it's usually with the intention of doing and saying less to get chores done. It isn't until the sticker chart is up for a while that parents realize they are actually required to do more than before. Not only do they still need to nag their children into performing their chores, now the parents have to keep score!

> It's not whether you win or lose, it's how you place the blame.
> –Oscar Wilde

It doesn't take long to resent this additional effort, supporting a program that can only work when parents are so involved. Those saddle sores from riding the horse are still there. When the program eventually fails, the parent blames the program, the child or even herself. The child, however, has only one place to go with his feelings: inside. He will internalize his parent's resentment and feel frustrated, guilty and inadequate, even if he outwardly blames you. The child will believe the failure is all his fault but won't know how to make things better.

STARTING POINTS

In the previous chapters you've had the opportunity to stand back and reflect on yourself. You've done exercises that uncovered your true objectives and your current mental programming. You've developed an outline of the actions that will teach responsibility to your children. But as important as all that is, it's still only half the equation. Before you can move on you must also consider where your children are starting. Looking at your current and past behavior modification methods will help you understand how much unlearning your children will need to go through before the new empowered actions you want from them begin to manifest.

> Management by objective works—if you know the objectives. Ninety percent of the time you don't. –Peter Drucker

WHOSE JOB IS IT ANYWAY?

Children generally want to do the things their parents want them to do; they just don't believe that they are actually responsible to decide when these things need to be done. For example, Tommy may know he needs to make his bed, brush his teeth and feed the hamster every morning. They are his regular tasks and Tommy understands his job is to do these things. Tommy's mother wants to help him, so she tells Tommy when to start, reminds Tommy

> *I know that you believe you understand what you think I said, but I'm not sure you realize that what you heard is not what I meant.*
> *—Robert McCloskey*

to get busy "doing," reminds Tommy that it's almost time to leave, reminds Tommy that he still needs to brush his teeth, reminds Tommy … you get the picture. Tommy doesn't believe that he is responsible to decide *when* to act because Tommy's mom does that for him by reminding him over and over. The key here is that children simply don't think they are actually responsible for the outcome because there is someone telling them what to do and when to do it. If Tommy's mom doesn't raise her voice or express any disappointment in this arrangement, then Tommy feels great and is happy in his success because, even if his mother reminded him twenty times, he feels his success is only measured by the *doing* of the tasks. We know, however, that at some point Tommy's mom will show disappointment, stress and displeasure in her need to be so actively involved in Tommy's chores. While Tommy isn't keeping track of his mother's reminders, Tommy's mother *is*— and with growing feelings of impatience. She wants Tommy to do his chores without her, and Tommy just thinks he needs to do his chores. Do you see the difference? To give Tommy a sticker reward is meaningless as a motivator unless Tommy knows how to act *on his own*. Without empowering a child to initiate action on his own, the feeling of accountability remains limited only to the task itself.

A NEW YORK MINUTE

Another factor at work here is the complete lack of understanding on the child's part about how time moves and feels. Children experience so many feelings and have so many distractions in every minute of every day that the way time feels is in a constant state of flux. When they are playing their favorite game, ten minutes flies by; when they are sitting quietly in church, ten minutes feels like an eternity. There isn't a uniform feeling to time or an anchor from which to make decisions.

With current programs the parent provides a list of chores on a page or chart and explains to the child what is expected. Often the list of chores spans the entire day—morning chores listed the same as evening chores. From the parent's perspective, the list gives the child all the information needed for success and ample time in which to complete everything. The child knows:

- What to do

- How to do it

- Where to do it

- When it's to be done ... Or does he?

The parent walks away brushing her hands and believing she has given her child the tools needed to get all the jobs done. Great! *Ah, finally Tommy*

Is time moving at the same speed for this boy?

will do his chores without me nagging! The problem isn't with the tasks or even with who is responsible to do the tasks; it's the *when* part that causes Tommy's problem.

I'm not suggesting that when a parent gives a list of tasks to a child and tells him to do the chores today, for example, that the child can't understand this implies the *when*—sometime between waking up and the time he goes to bed. Clearly it does. And I'll go further and assume the child is willing to do the chores on the list. He gets started and—Wham!—out of nowhere comes a distraction. He sees the perfect Lego piece for the model he's been working on, a random daydream gets underway, a rehearsal of an upcoming conversation begins, etc. In his mind he intended to only give that distraction a minute or two of attention before going right back to his chores. But before he knew what happened, his parent is standing in front of him tapping a toe in frustration. "Why aren't you dressed yet? We have to leave for school now." Not only was the timing of each task vague, the mechanism for teaching the concept of time was missing. That minute or two in the morning, while feeling to the child exactly like a minute or two, becomes fifteen in the blink of an eye. Once the parent steps in again, the whole process spirals downward.

I'm not sure anyone can teach another person the *feeling* of time. Perception is unique. Showing a child a clock and teaching him how to tell time aren't the same things. It may be that understanding the feeling of time won't happen until later in life for him. Until then, the Morning Peacemaker's specific and limited time parameters and its use of snooze timers successively progress the child's skills for time management so he can be successful as he discovers his own unique feeling of time. He will be given a set of multi-function kitchen timers preset by you for either five- or ten-minute intervals. Each time the timer signals the passing of five or ten minutes, the child experiences another variation of the speed of time while having his focus redirected without your intervention. In this safe environment the child is free to experiment with independence. As the child gains experience and confidence using the pre-set timers, he begins to connect his body's rhythm with his mind.

By initially limiting the task list to the morning hours, the child is given a chance to practice prioritizing a small number of familiar tasks with understandable and natural boundaries. The timing is perfect because it is clearly and naturally defined. The purpose of completing all tasks by the time everyone leaves for the day establishes an acceptable and reasonable expectation. Also, in the event a parent is tortured by her urges to "help just a little," she needs only to control herself for a short period of time.

Let's use the example of the sippy cup again to see how we employ these techniques in other ways. The use of the sippy cup begins in the kitchen over an easy-to-clean floor, which limits the time for your child's practice to only that time spent in the kitchen. At first only small amounts of water are put into the cup, which limits the amount of water for which the child is responsible. Finally, the tight lids on those cups actually make getting liquid out of them nearly impossible. That was the "training wheel" that allowed everyone to relax because there was little room to make any big mistakes. I remember the sippy cup and the spills I cleaned at first. Though annoying, I was motivated to support my children because I knew they needed to spill a few drinks to learn how to manage the cup. Quickly, they mastered the skill just as they mastered their morning chores; I no longer sit in the kitchen with paper towels at the ready and I no longer nag my boys to get their morning chores done. (Psst—I also remind them less and less about other responsibilities during other parts of the day—even homework. But I'll get to that later.) (Psst again—they even set their timers for other tasks on their own…Later, I promise.)

Reality check: The timer is a tool, just like training wheels and sippy cups; but it isn't any more magical than anything else, so expect a learning period that includes a few spills as your child figures it all out.

Apron Strings

Parents aren't the only ones who have trouble letting go. It's a tall order to initiate action on your own as a child. Depending on his age, a child may have had little opportunity or encouragement to act on his own before. Self-starting is even discouraged most of the time. What would your reaction be to your budding self-starter when he decided to "help" you paint the kitchen as a surprise? Chances are good that it would discourage any future attempts at "helping" like that. At the very least, you would tell your child to ask permission first. When it came time for the child to assume some responsibilities in the house again, it might take him a while to believe he is ready and to trust that, if he makes a mistake (like the kitchen mess) his parents won't be angry.

While we might see a big difference between self-starting a bed-making project and self-starting a kitchen-painting project, the child may not see too much difference because both will feel risky at first. Children will have a difficult time rewiring their years of programming that taught them to wait for help or instruction. As parents, we know our children will be happy when they are successful, and we often orchestrate events to ensure their success. We do this

> *Too often we give children answers to remember rather than problems to solve.*
> *–Roger Lewin*

in many ways to boost their confidence and to fuel their ambition for more. It's a great technique to get the child going, because success usually breeds more success. The rub comes when it's time to pass the reins, because current behavior-modification programs don't provide a transition mechanism. Until the Peacemaker Parent, it was nag or no nag, making it feel risky for both parent and child.

Here Today, Gone Tomorrow

Some parents venture into to the no-nag zone cold turkey. Thinking back to the cart-and-horse example, this means that one minute the parent is riding the horse, business as usual, and the next minute she has jumped off, leaving the child stuck in the cart waiting for something to happen. This sudden reversal after years of support won't work for either party, even if the child knows in advance that, starting tomorrow, you won't be reminding him to do his chores. The child will struggle with the sudden independence and will invariably miss a few tasks on the list. Though the parent decided to stop nagging, she probably had not stopped expecting short-term results. As the child fails to produce those results, the parent's message of disappointment is sent out loud and clear.

These parents, full of initial resolve to zip their lips, are likely to crumble at the sight of a child sitting on the edge of the bed with one sock on and the other in hand, eyes glazed over and looking off in the distance, completely distracted by an adventure happening in a galaxy far, far away. The urge to get the child moving again is overwhelming. Thinking, "He's so close to making it and he'll feel so proud when he does," unconscious programming overrides their conscious resolve and they step in. Standing outside the bedroom door in this scenario won't seem like nagging. These parents don't realize, however, that they are standing on a slippery slope. Oh how quickly one small reminder turns into a few and then, before you know it, you end up right back where you started, but with an extra layer of programming to undo.

> *The quickest way for a parent to get a child's attention is to sit down and look comfortable.*

When this scenario plays out a few times, the child learns that with each new sticker chart he should just sit tight because his parent will eventually jump back on the horse. It's confusing, to say the least, and chips away at the child's self confidence.

When you begin using the Peacemaker Parent's Morning Peacemaker approach, remember your history and stay strong through this period of time. It will take a while for children to realize that it's ok to try things on their own and that you really aren't going to jump back on the horse this time. If you've jumped off and on many times, they are likely to wait even longer before they slowly climb out of the cart and stand looking at the horse. They may even holler for you from the cart: "Mom, what am I supposed to do, again?" or "Wait! You didn't tell me we were leaving so soon! I haven't eaten breakfast yet!" Only when they are sure you mean business will they start trying to get the horse moving on their own.

One Hit Wonder

A child will have tremendous difficulty mastering self-motivation without support as he practices these new techniques. I call this "supported empowerment," and it is central to the calendar pages, snooze timers and reviews used in the Morning Peacemaker. Success is easy when someone else tells you what to do, someone else reminds you and someone else keeps track of your results. But this is really only a success in following orders. What happens when no one is willing to give orders or an order is given only once? It's easy to imagine the results, and I think it safe to say that teachers, roommates, employers, spouses, etc., won't want to work as hard as you do to support your child.

Being able to decide one's own responsibilities and to redirect one's focus after distractions are critical skills needed for achievement in all areas of life, and they need to be practiced. Throughout our lives we are confronted with distractions; advertisers are masters at steeling our attention away from reality. The lure of entertainment and good times constantly threatens to redirect us from our goals. Many would-be successful people were simply unable to sustain focus or unable to redirect their attention when it wandered. By using the Peacemaker approach, your child will have a head-start in learning how to master goal setting and goal achieving because he will have practiced. In the book *The Outliers: A Story of Success*, Michael Gladwell makes the claim that it takes approximately 10,000 hours of practice to develop mastery in a skill. 10,000 hours! Even if that figure is off by a hundred or so hours, mastery will take some time to achieve. The earlier your child starts practicing, the sooner he will become a master. How much farther can he go in life if he can hit the ground running his first year in college?

Front and Center

Behavior modification charts have been around for a long time. Without much deviation, chart designers today have continued the standard grid-like design with the days of the week across the top of the grid and the list of chores to be done down the left side. While there are ways to dress up the presentation, at the end of the day you have a grid front and center.

One Size Does NOT Fit All

With the advancements in computer technology and the Internet, you can now find some options online. *My Reward Board* is one such option. From the creators of the educational software Jump Start, this interactive chart can be used on your home computer. The company has added color and animated graphics that encourage the child's interaction, and provides some preset options for customizing the display. The website also provides some ideas for parents and gives a lengthy list of task options from which to choose. For $19.95 you can run *My Reward Board* on three computers in your home. Though *My Reward Board* offers some preset options to customize the display, and a few other bells and whistles, it's still just another (albeit fancier) version of the same old grid.

No matter how visually exciting any pre-designed chart might be in the beginning, without personalizing the program for your child the excitement will quickly fade and the chart, along with the whole program, will just blend into the wall. So what do you do? What will make the chart or display capture your child's attention time and time again? The only answer is: your child. Only pictures of him or things for which he has a passion will grab hold of him over and over again. Remember, he is in a normal developmental stage that makes him self-centered. A chart decorated with footballs will bore even the most devoted football fanatic eventually. Without customizing those footballs so that they are reflections of him, his interest will dwindle and die.

Thinking Outside the Box

As a child I used to push Brussels sprouts around my plate in an effort to convince my mother that I had eaten some of the portion she gave me. I really disliked Brussels sprouts, and it looked like less to me when they weren't all clumped together. Sadly, my mother was rarely fooled by my ploy. But

I found this strategy to be effective with my son Jack's task list. After initial success with the calendar pages, Jack began to fail. At reviews, he wouldn't really be able to say why he wasn't as successful as he had been in the beginning so we just kept going, thinking things would work themselves out again. After about three weeks of difficulty he and I had a special meeting to figure out strategies. He said he just felt overwhelmed by all the chores and had given up trying. Understand there were eight tasks on the page at that time and one of them was marking the calendar page.

Tuesday May 6, 2008

- Make Bed
- Get Dressed
- PJ's Away
- Eat Breakfast
- Brush Teeth & Hair
- Backpack 8:35
- Calendar Page

Figure 1

The only real chores were: bed, pjs, dressed, teeth, hair, breakfast and backpack. After we talked about the tasks and agreed they were all needed, he held up one of his pages and said exasperatedly, "But just *look* at it all. It's too much!" Figure 1 is a copy of the page he showed me. Notice that the task list is in a column down the left side. I realized in that moment that Jack was not a linear thinker like Michael and I. When he saw a neatly aligned list it overwhelmed his feelings because it looked like so much all clumped together. Remembering my experience with Brussels sprouts, I offered to push the tasks around the page to make it look like less. Figure 2 is a sample of his re-designed page. The same tasks are listed; but by making this little change, he was able to resume his previous successes.

Jack was overwhelmed by seeing all his chores clumped together. Neither one of us knew his brain processed visually this way before then, but knowing this now has empowered him in far-reaching ways. He was relieved because he then understood that

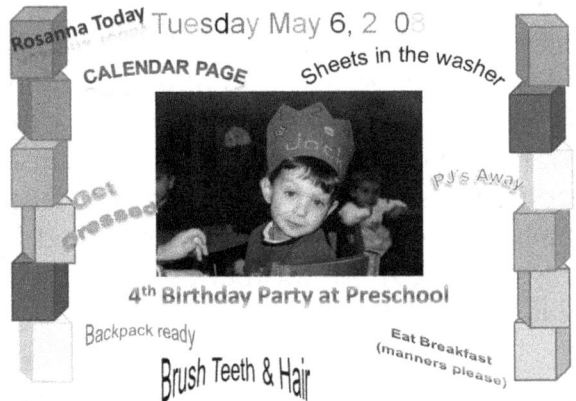

Rosanna Today Tuesday May 6, 2 08

CALENDAR PAGE   Sheets in the washer

Get dressed   PJ's Away

4th Birthday Party at Preschool

Backpack ready   Eat Breakfast (manners please)

Brush Teeth & Hair

Figure 2

similar overwhelming feelings from other situations were connected to his need for less clumping. On his own he developed strategies to ease the problem, such as with math homework. When presented with a page of math problems lined in columns he now covers some of the columns with extra paper to make it feel less overwhelming. He will use this knowledge throughout his life, and it all started with eight tasks rearranged on a page. I am thankful that I could think outside the box—the grid box, that is—to make small changes and create a unique presentation that has given Jack a leg-up on life. Michael, however, did not want to change his task list presentation. Because he is a linear thinker he knew a random presentation would overwhelm him. Though Michael's presentation didn't change, he too benefited from the experience because it opened his mind to the possibilities of creating options when things don't work in their original form.

Let's imagine for a minute that I was using a pre-designed sticker chart with my linear and non-linear thinkers. The success rate would have been fifty percent because only one of them could process information in the linear format. What, then, for Jack? I would have thought the problems were with him; it wouldn't have occurred to me that the linear presentation was a factor, since I am a linear thinker myself and Michael was successful with the linear design. Everyone, including poor Jack, would have begun to think he had a problem, when the real problem was with the chart. I wonder how many times this happens in homes all over the world, and how many children feel inadequate needlessly. Michael and Jack now aren't as quick to find themselves lacking when a situation is difficult. Rather, they look for creative ways to make the situation better for themselves.

THE FREEDOM OF A FRESH START

The best thing about the future is that it comes only a day at a time.

–Abraham Lincoln

Charts now are created to span as little as a few days to as much as even a month's worth of chores. Perhaps the design was to reduce the parent's effort in maintaining the chart or simply to fill all the space available. Starting fresh on Monday, you and your child would see rows and columns of things waiting to be done every day. Ugh—a bit daunting, I think. It's difficult to think about one day or one task at a time this way. As the week progresses and stickers are filled in the grid squares, each time anyone looks at the chart he not only sees the current day's results, he also sees the previous days' as well. While the parent may want to look back through the week tracking trends or highlighting progress, the child doesn't. When he looks at the chart all the child sees are reminders of his failures yesterday or the day before. Even the parent gets sucked into that downer because her current unconscious programming is to look for failure rather than success.

Think honestly for a minute. When you look at a chart aren't you first looking for the things that didn't get done? It's a downer, not an upper; and people are much more likely to try harder and do more when they feel good. Looking back is critical to finding out which strategies work and which don't; it just isn't productive to do it every day. You must avoid this trap and treat each new day as a fresh start. With the Morning Peacemaker, a fresh page greets your child every morning. It's a clean slate presented with a positive image of your child, front and center. Uplifted right from the gate, your child has the freedom to start anew and try again.

> *If you build it, they will come.*
> *–Field of Dreams*

ORDER UP!

When you look at the lengthy list of task choices offered by the third-party producers of charts, not only are there too many to choose from but so many are subjective. When presented with the endless list of choices you can put on your child's task list, it seems like the chart makers are giving you the opportunity to order up the child of your dreams. "I'll take bed maker, dishwasher, health consciousness, honesty, politeness, well groomed, homework doer ..." And why stop there when you can just sprinkle on "nice to sibling" and "toy tidier" too? Sure, we want our children to be all these things and more. But you're not in a restaurant. It's really hard to maintain a simple approach when the marketers of these charts and programs want to sell you on the idea of their magic. Resist the temptation to get it all in from the start; it is the saboteur sneaking in. Besides, you don't need anyone to tell you what your child should do, and only you know what he is ready to do.

> *People have a way of becoming what you encourage them to be, not what you nag them to be.*
> *–Unknown*

SHADES OF GREY

Included on so many charts are "chores" that are not clear and objective. They require a judgment call by either your child or you in order to determine compliance. For example, how do you measure politeness? Is it just saying "please" or is "thank you" required too? Does it count if you had to remind him to say it to the grocery clerk? How do you measure "nice"? Is it not hitting your sister or is it always including your sister in play too? Does it count if he isn't "nice" but has a reason? How do you measure "respectful"? Is it addressing adults with "Mr." or "Mrs." or is it not calling another child a name also? Does it count if she is shy and hides behind you when you're talking to another adult? These "chores" aren't really chores; they are values. And when charts list subjective values there can be a whole lot of confusion. The ability to understand values depends greatly upon the age of the child. A young child may not have the maturity or experience to control impulses while he connects these values to behavior. Combine this with the infinite number of times and combinations these values apply in a single day and you have a big, scary, grey cloud.

> *The happiest people in the world are those who feel absolutely terrific about themselves, and this is the natural outgrowth of accepting total responsibility for every part of their life.* –Brian Tracy

ASK ME NO QUESTIONS AND I'LL TELL YOU NO LIES

Including values on a sticker chart forces both you and your child to judge his performance greatly. Even the most consistent among us will have good days and bad days that affect our judgments. One day you may think a stormy look from your daughter is disrespectful and another you may see it as her using self-control by not saying something disrespectful. Your judgment will often be subject to your mood at the time. Listing values on a sticker chart also promotes dishonesty and excuse-making in the child. You may not understand how serious your child takes the concept of honesty, for example. A child may be conflicted because to be nice to someone might make it necessary to be dishonest. What's the message? It's ok to be dishonest if it means you're nice? Or are you damned if you do and damned if you don't? I know that, as adults, we sometimes wrestle with situational ethics, but a child isn't experienced enough or mature enough to be confronted with it on a sticker chart.

And how about the times you aren't around to witness an act of "disrespect" at school? The child remembers it but you're not counting it because you don't know about it. Is the message to the child, then, that it will only count against him if he is caught? Or are you expecting him to disclose his mistakes fully for the reckoning?

Teaching your child to be honest, respectful, nice and so on creates a solid, happy adult, and these values go hand-in-hand with being responsible and accountable. While the lessons must be taught, the mistake comes when a parent believes he can order them up on a sticker chart. To be honest and respectful requires confidence and high self-esteem first. When you are able to teach your children how they can be responsible and accountable in the morning, the foundation for their moral behavior is created. They build confidence because they realize that learning takes mistakes, and now mistakes mean opportunities for building strategies, not a reflection of their worth.

> *At college-age, you can tell who is best at taking tests and going to school, but you can't tell who the best people are. That worries the hell out of me.*
> *–Barnaby C. Keeney*

Honesty comes about when your child believes that his mistakes won't cause you to think the worst about him. He is, therefore, free to tell you everything because he knows you aren't judging his character. He will approach new tasks and situations with confidence, knowing he is expected to get it wrong a bit while he figures out how to achieve the results he wants. Self-esteem follows when the child has figured it out, because he believes in his ability to repeat his success. The child with high self-esteem won't need to exclude another child from play or follow the lead of a child who isn't being nice in order to get what he wants. The child can be nice and helpful to others because he believes in his ability to create the results he wants.

HAPPINESS LINGERS

Be pleasant until ten o'clock in the morning and the rest of the day will take care of itself.

–Elbert Hubbard

There is a direct relationship between the way days start and the way they end up. Starting out feeling good inside is like dressing in a suit of armor that shields you from negative thoughts and emotions. With this protection you are more able to greet people, tasks, events, etc., with an open mind. You're more apt to say "yes" to things and agree to cooperate with others just because you feel good.

I'm sure you can think of a time when you performed a random act of kindness just because you felt good inside. Think back to a time when something really great happened. Maybe it was getting into the college of your choice, beginning a new romantic relationship that was awesome or hearing you were going to become a parent. I'm sure that, for a time after that uplifting moment, it was nearly impossible to bring you down. If you spilled a drink you were able to laugh it off; if something else didn't turn out as you had hoped you were able to make peace with it more easily: "That's ok, because I'm so excited about my new job!"

> *Humor helps us to think out of the box. The average child laughs about 400 times a day; the average adult laughs only 15 times a day. What happened to the other 385 laughs?* –*Unknown*

Remember being able to bounce back fully functional at work the day after a late night out with your new boyfriend or girlfriend? Your happiness transcended even sleep deprivation! It was almost as if nothing else mattered because you were so delighted. When someone tells you he has good news and bad news, he usually gives you the good news first to minimize the impact the bad news will have on you. (If people don't do that for you now, ask for it that way in the future. It really helps.) When you start the day happy you have a better shot at staying happy.

Adults have a variety of ways to start a day out right: meditation, music, funny morning talk shows, exercise, daily comic strip calendars, etc. Conversely, many a tough day started out with waking up late and rushing out the door. I'm less likely to let a fellow driver merge into traffic in front of me on days like that. While I'm pretending not to notice this poor fellow, I'm hugging the bumper of the car in front of me so closely that I smell the driver's coffee. I'm pissed off in general and go through all this aggravation just to be one car-length ahead of the other driver on the highway. After I win that battle (ha!), I'm sure to find other battles all day long.

THE INDISPENSABLE YOU

There is no way a third party can customize a program with enough uniqueness to capture every child. Only you can do that. And while it might sound like a tall order, it truly isn't. At the end of the book I've included easy step-by-step instructions that walk you through the process of creating unique calendar pages using Microsoft PowerPoint. For those of you not familiar with computers or this software program, do not lose heart; you will learn the basics of how to use these computer tools, and the basics are all you need. If the anticipation of this still puts you off, consider this: How much time and money are you wasting now trying to make the square shape of a generic sticker chart fit the round shape of your child? Only you can create the right portrayal that epitomizes your child. Only you know enough about him and only you witness the changes through which he goes to enable the attention grabber to keep pace with those changes. Only you.

THE GIFT THAT KEEPS ON GIVING

There is a big bonus for you in all of this also. Each morning, as your child is uplifted by his image, you will also be uplifted. It's obvious that we tend only to take pictures of the best of times; we generally only record the high points, right? As you select the pictures for each page you are given the opportunity to relive those great moments. I find myself excited to see their reaction to each day's new page image. It's like giving them a present they unwrap every morning. It makes me happy to know they will start each day being reminded of how awesome they are. And it doesn't stop there. In my family, my husband, Ralph, is the one to commute to work each day. His nine-to-five is really a six-thirty to seven most of the time. He sacrifices so much time being away from the boys and me; in fact, all too often, he is up and out of the house before the boys are even awake. For him, those daily calendar pages help sustain his connection to them. He, too, is uplifted. He walks out the door in the morning with a smile and a renewed resolve that his sacrifices are for a great cause. You can't get that from any generic sticker chart, fancy or otherwise.

THE TAKE AWAY

Be realistic about where you are now so that you have an understanding of the behaviors you might see pop up as you implement the Peacemaker Parent's Morning Peacemaker approach. Trust in your resolve, because it will take time. There will be many times your child will test the limits of your patience and the truth of your words. When these things happen see them as steps in the right direction. Actions speak louder than words. No one understands that more than children. They need to see you walk-the-talk, so to speak. When your actions match what you've said (e.g., they aren't punished for taking action, you aren't stepping in with reminders and you're not angry when they make a mistake), then they will relax and show you what magic really looks like.

CHAPTER SIX

Setting Up the Morning Peacemaker

The will to succeed is important, but what's even more important is the will to prepare.

–Bobby Knight

After all your mental prep work and the conceptualization of the previous chapters, it's time to put the rubber to the road, so to speak. You should feel very excited to be poised and ready to get started, knowing your efforts will bear fruit. With your resolve and clear understanding of what it takes to accomplish your objectives, you will succeed in establishing peace in your home. There are only two simple steps to take before you can roll out the Morning Peacemaker fully: The first is planning the initial meeting; the second is preparing your child. You're just two steps from the pot of gold, and the good news is you are halfway through the first one.

STEP ONE: PLANNING THE MEETING

As part of Chapter Four, you thought through the program and developed a soft outline of your child's task list, the review schedule and his incentives. All that's left is to get specific about the actual meeting by preparing yourself, creating the visual aids and drafting an agenda.

Use the chronological outline below as a template for your agenda, omitting the prep work and filling in specific details from your soft outline. You'll use the agenda in your rollout meeting, as a checklist and as a place to take notes. Even though you'll incorporate your child's ideas into the program, it's smart to have suggestions ready from which to start a dialogue.

> *A carelessly planned project takes three times longer to complete than expected; a carefully planned project takes only twice as long.*
> *–Unknown*

THE PEACE PLAN

1. Setting the Stage

    a. Plan for peace—2 weeks out

        i. Talk about peace / talk about team

        ii. Fun and games before

            1. Confidence-building exercises (pouring drinks, toasting bread)

    b. Point out positives—1 week out

2. "D" Day—The Rollout Meeting

    a. When—After lunch but before dinner

    b. Environment—Fiddling and focused (puzzle, Lego, coloring, action figures)

    c. Refreshments (something small and low in sugar)

    d. Maximum time—15 to 30 minutes guaranteed

3. The Morning of the First Meeting

    a. Happy, easy morning, little or no TV

    b. Repeat praises

        i. Getting older / ready for more responsibility

        ii. Build confidence with examples

4. Be Ready with Answers to Questions He Might Ask

    a. What tasks are important?

    b. Why are they important?

    c. Why the morning?

5. The Calendar Page / It's All About HIM!

    a. Every day a new picture and a fresh start

    b. Best design for your child

        i. Design options from you

        ii. Design options from him (paper, pencils, markers, crayons)

    c. How to use the calendar page

        i. Check off things when done

            1. Only his hand

            2. Where it will go, start and finish

        ii. Feel great (anything missed gets done later)

6. Working with Time

    a. 1 hour / 5 or 10 minutes at a time

    b. How long for each task (and a little extra, just in case)

    c. Back into the start of the morning

7. The Snooze Timers—The Automatic Reminders

    a. Snooze buttons

    b. Turning off one snooze is the start of the next

8. Incentives

    a. Current salary, allowance of any sort (i.e., money, screen time, stickers, treats, etc.)

    b. Base salary plus commission bonus

    c. Your child chooses how to be paid. Stay with allowance or switch to commission

9. Review and Payout Meetings—Negotiate and Compromise

    a. How did the week go? Are changes needed?

    b. Your child should want to attend because:

        i. Pay day!

        ii. Equal voice in creating the best system

        iii. His time to voice his opinions and ideas

        iv. Opportunity to ask questions and get help

    c. When? Each week for 2 months

    d. Where? The same place as the initial meeting

    e. How long? 15 to 30 minutes guaranteed

10. Ready, Set—GO!

    a. Grace period: Try it for "free" for a few weeks

    b. When everyone is ready, it goes "live"

11. Pledge

    a. You go first, "I promise ..."

        i. Not to nag you in the morning.

        ii. I'll listen and cooperate with your ideas.

        iii. I'll be happy with your best effort—really.

        iv. I'll remember you are trying your best.

        v. I'll see mistakes as opportunities to learn.

        vi. I'll stick with the deal.

    b. He goes second—he may need some help here:

        i. To do his best every day.

        ii. To stay positive.

iii. To believe in himself.

iv. To remember he is learning something and it takes time.

v. To not push for too much, so he can meet his pledge.

It's An Investment

"Opportunity is missed by most people because it is dressed in overalls and looks like work."

–Thomas Alva Edison

Your worthy objectives require your worthy efforts. No matter how you slice it, you just can't get something for nothing. I realize I'm restating this issue; however, it's just so important that you keep in mind the need for your effort. Though implementing this program isn't by any means difficult, it will require some effort on your part. It's easy to succumb to slick marketing that promises big returns on low investments, because it would just be so great to have someone else fix everything for you: a pill to lose weight, a cream to erase wrinkles or a chart to teach responsibility, for example. We know these things don't exist. If you want to lose weight you must do something different today than you were doing yesterday. Just as starting that new fitness regime requires prep work, so does the Peacemaker program. For the fitness program, you'll educate yourself about nutrition, talk to your doctor, research gym memberships and exercise programs that fit your goals, etc. Those are the first steps that set the stage for your action. When you begin eating and exercising according to your plan, the foundation you created through your prep work will support you when the going gets rough—and the going always gets a little rough before you see improvements. For example, during your research you learn that a plain bagel roughly equals five slices of bread in calories and carbohydrates! Wouldn't knowing that fact make it easier to choose a different snack when you start to reach for that bagel?

> *Basic research is what I am doing when I don't know what I'm doing.*
> *–Wernher von Braun*

SETTING THE STAGE

The month before rollout, there is a simple process you'll go through as you set the stage for the Morning Peacemaker. You start by quietly looking for ways to strengthen your child's self-esteem and begin the reprogramming process for both of you. You'll practice your new way of thinking and start to look for ways you can help him connect his actions to his results. Take a week or so to practice quietly while you look for ideas. I needed a bit more than a week to get things straight in my mind.

> *I am extraordinarily patient, provided I get my own way in the end.*
> *–Margaret Thatcher*

Once you're set, you'll start pointing out his positive actions and results. Watch as this gently shifts his thinking and supports your new resolve. How much time you spend in this stage will depend on your history of past attempts to change behavior. For me, two weeks in advance of the rollout worked well. We all had some reprogramming to do, but it didn't take long. If you know there is much to unlearn for your child—and for you—then allow a little more time. Some things just can't be rushed.

During this period you are preparing yourself just as much as you are preparing your child. Your conscious, positive attention as you look for opportunities to praise and acknowledge your child's efforts begin to reprogram your thinking, as well as his. As you practice looking for good things to praise you will begin to see just how much good there really is already. Chip by chip the layers of your old programming will begin to fall away and your conscious effort to find the good will become an unconscious habit. Your glass of cranberry juice will be mostly water before you know it.

STEP TWO, "BY THE WAY..."

Conversations during the preparation phase are all about teamwork. Small, positive comments at opportune times are all that are needed and, in

> *Many attempts to communicate are nullified by saying too much.*
> *–Robert Greenleaf*

fact, are all that will probably get through to your child anyway. Your child won't listen to any message if it's packaged in a lengthy monologue. Keep your messages short and simple. Comments that connect his individual efforts to the success of the family team will show him he has an important role in the family. For ex-ample, when you see him turn off a light, mention in a by-the-way manor that every time he does that the family can use the money saved to help pay for a night at the movies. Show him that his efforts make a big difference. Through seemingly random comments you'll begin to help him connect his role in making the house run smoothly and peacefully.

It's important to comment only on the good things he does that benefit the fam-ily; pointing out any of his actions that drain the family will turn him off and keep him feeling disempowered. Those types of negative comments will strengthen the old programming that you're trying to change. Here are a few more ideas for positive, by-the-way sound bytes:

> *A blow with a word strikes deeper than a blow with a sword.*
> *–Robert Burton*

- When he puts clean clothes in his drawer, not the hamper, it means you'll have more time to play together because there is less laundry work for you.

- When he puts his dirty clothes in the hamper, it means there is more time to play together because now you have less tidy-up work.

- When he puts the couch pillows back on the couch, it means that friends will be encouraged to visit more because they'll feel welcome in a tidy house.

- When he helps to shovel snow, it means more time for a snowball fight!

These by-the-way sound bytes about cause and effect link your child's positive actions to the positive effects he creates. That's powerful stuff and he will gobble every tidbit you hand him.

When he begins to understand how much his efforts contribute to the family he begins to own a piece of the positive results. He begins to recog-nize how important his role is and will rise up to do more because you're recognizing it. Your child then feels the power he has to make things great for everyone. You'll know that the message is getting through when he starts talking about his great efforts to help the family. When he comes to you and says he's helped you by hanging up the bathroom towel, think "Bingo! We're on the right track!"

As your child responds to your praise it's time to broaden the scope of your cause-and-effect messages by connecting your role and responsibilities to him. The passing remarks I make to my boys are always positive and laced with the joy I have in being their mother. For example, "We sure would be hungry if I hadn't made time to cook dinner." "Boy, I'm glad I wrote a note to remind me to pick you up from practice early." If one of them wanted my attention while I was preparing dinner, I would say, "I wish I could come now but I have my job to do first. It's my job to make sure dinner is ready on time so we won't get grouchy from being too hungry." Later, at dinner, I'd say how glad I am that I didn't stop for play before I got dinner ready, because I am really hungry. I might add an extra "thank you" if my son pitched in to help and might tell him how awesome it was to be able to play more because he helped me. Some other suggestions for personalizing your efforts to your child's happiness are:

- Because you did the laundry on time, it means that he can wear his favorite shirt to school.

- Because you went to the grocery store, it means that he has tasty lunches and snacks for school.

- Because you stopped to get gas in the car earlier in the day, it means that he is on time for karate.

The Garden

Many times I use nature as an analogy to create understanding. Applying this analogy to the Peacemaker Parent method I want you to imagine yourself the creator of a beautiful garden. The garden you create will be filled with energy, promise, possibility and beauty. There is only one plant that grows here: a vine that loops and meanders as it grows, until it occupies every part of the garden space. The mature vine will be lush and green, the very picture of strength and lasting beauty. Though slow to produce buds, once a bud does appear the flower is quick to follow. The vine will be in a constant state of bloom, though at different points along its winding body. The flowers are magnificent and attract attention from everything and everyone near the garden. All are drawn to the awesome spectacle of the vine in bloom.

The fruit that replaces the flower is even more powerful than the flower. While the flowers are the reward for those drawn to the garden, the fruit sustains the vine. The fruit provides the vine with energy so that it can repeat its awesome spectacle again and again in other places in the garden. While one section of the vine is in its glory, the other sections are at rest, waiting their turn to bring forth their magic. Imagine this garden for a moment. You are the gardener and you plant only one kind of seed—the *Yes You Can* seed. Your child is the vine and, with your nurturing, these seeds create their beautiful *Yes I Can* vine.

In the beginning the vine is vulnerable to pollution. Impurities in the seeds or water will delay its growth. Over- or under-tending will also set it back and may even stunt the full growth potential of the vine. Tender and deliberate care must be given to ensure that only the finest seeds and water reach the garden. The soil must be wholesome and balanced.

Your presence is needed in the garden at all times, though your location in it will change as it grows. At first you will be right in the middle, casting seeds by the handfuls to all corners. You will be wading in the mud as you water the garden and pull the weeds that threaten to take root. The job is very hands-on at first and you'll get messy and tired from the work. Some days you'll think it's too much effort or you'll want to let someone else take over for a while. But it's your job and you must tend the garden. Oh sure, others can help; but you are the one responsible. You must inspect everything before it goes into the garden to be sure that only careful helpers use the purest seeds and water.

> *Your mind is a garden, your thoughts are the seeds, the harvest can be either flowers or weeds.*
> *–Unknown*

As the vine begins to grow it will start to push you out. The small vines are delicate and cannot be stepped on, so you will have less and less space to walk. As it covers more ground you're pushed out farther and farther to the edges of the space until, one day, you can only tend the garden from outside the space. Once outside the garden you become the recipient of its glory. Its flowers and fruit will astound you and fill you with pride in the role you played in the vine's creation.

In the early stages of planting the *Yes You Can* seeds, it may be difficult to picture the magnificent *Yes I Can* vine. The condition of the garden space when you begin will determine how long it will take to prepare the soil

> *I guess a good gardener starts as a good weeder.*
> *–Amos Pettingill*

to accept the seeds. The ground may be hard and littered with bits of paper and weeds that you'll have to remove. This can be especially true when the soil was struck by disaster or left unattended for a while. The conditions in the garden must be right for the vine to grow to its full potential. The going can be slow. It will be some time before you see evidence of growth on the surface, but you must always believe in your duty and remain focused on your success.

The *Yes You Can* seeds you cast around the garden are the small comments you make and the activities you orchestrate prior to rolling out this program. You are preparing your child so he will believe in himself enough to try what you ask him to try. He won't know consciously what you're up to, but his feelings inside will respond. The seeds you are planting will grow.

THE OUCH, THE SILVER LINING AND THE STRATEGY

As important as it is to point out all the positive things you do to make him happy, I think it almost more powerful for you to point out some of

> *Three Rules of Work:*
> *Out of clutter, find simplicity;*
> *From discord, find harmony;*
> *In the middle of difficulty, lies opportunity. –Albert Einstein.*

the mistakes you make to your child. Don't point out the mistakes that have a negative impact on him specifically; just keep the admission of your mistakes and their effects confined to you. When you point one out, have three things ready to say about the effect the mistake has:

1. *Ouch*—the negative impact on you that day

2. *Silver Lining*—the brighter side

3. *Strategy*—how you'll prevent it in the future

For example, you are in the car pulling away from the house in the morning and you realize you forgot your lunch. First, you admit your mistake: "Darn it, I left my lunch on the counter." Then, without too much distress, tell him the ouch: "Well, I guess I'll be a little hungry today." The silver lining is: "At least I ate a nice breakfast and now I'll be looking forward to a great dinner and maybe even a bit more dessert tonight to make up for lunch." Finish off with the strategy, "I think I'll try putting my lunch on top of my shoes so I'll be sure to remember to bring it from now on."

Maintaining a positive attitude about a mistake you've made and talking about the strategy you'll use to prevent it from happening again will be a great example for your child. You'll also be able to use this example when

> *Setting an example is not the main means of influencing another, it is the only means.* —*Albert Einstein*

something similar happens to him as he starts the program. He'll be supported because he has seen that he's got good company in the mistake-making category. If you happen to be that rare individual who is completely organized, you might need to make up a few mistakes; but if you're like me, you will have at least a few genuine examples to use.

Use mistakes that happen at home so that he can identify with them easily. Mistakes you make at work or in your adult dealings might not have the same impact or might require too much explaining. All the comments must be really short little sound bytes that seem off-the-cuff. Here are a few ideas:

- Forgot to brush your teeth: OUCH—possible embarrassment because of bad breath today; SILVER LINING—at least I brushed last night, so it can't be too bad; STRATEGY—put toothbrush out the night before and have breath mints available if you forget again.

- The shirt you want to wear is dirty: OUCH—not getting to wear the outfit you wanted today; SILVER LINING—I look good anyway and I'll wear that shirt tomorrow; STRATEGY—do a load of laundry every day to make sure all my clothes are ready all the time.

- Left dishes in the sink and someone popped over unexpectedly: OUCH—embarrassment for having an untidy house today; SILVER LINING—the visitor is a good friend and understands that our messy kitchen today doesn't mean we are messy people; STRATEGY—always tidy right away because you never know when it will be important.

Though it might go without saying, I'll say it anyway: In the event your child's needs in the morning distracted you and you're thinking it was because of him you forgot your lunch, don't say it. You're setting up a program that will be teaching him accountability, so you must accept full accountability for yourself, too. If you blame him or other circumstances for a mistake you've made, you reinforce blame as an acceptable substitute for accountability. Resist it at all costs. Whose job was it to remember your lunch, anyway? That's right—yours. So let him watch as you accept the responsibility.

During this time it's critical that all your comments are short and positive. Am I restating the same messages you have read in countless other books? Probably, but good advice bears repeating. Short, simple, light, funny, positive and empowering. When you package your message in a small box wrapped in bright, happy paper your child will tear it open and treasure your gift. Delivering a lengthy monologue gives him a package he can't wait to return.

In the past when you've come out with cause-and-effect comments they were probably at times of anger or frustration as you pointed out a mistake and the negative impact it had on you or others. At times like this your high emotion is the only thing your child hears. Anger, frustration, guilt, inadequacy and disappointment all sound the same, and he is programmed to tune out thinking and tune into feeling bad or becoming defensive. This time, however, when you deliver your sound byte, it will be with positive emotions and comments. When you sit down to play cards or do a puzzle or switch on that movie, that's when you say how happy you are he folded his clean shirt rather than putting it in the laundry hamper for you to do. That's when you draw the connection from his actions to the positive results, and you do it while he is enjoying those results. Imagine how proud he will be the next time he resists the temptation to put a clean shirt in the laundry hamper and tells you that he helped you do the laundry!

THE RISK RUSH

Within a few days of setting the stage with sound bytes you will start handing the reins over to your child. Offer him the opportunity to do age-appropriate things he hasn't been allowed to do before. There are so many little things that have the potential for small, but harmless, disasters—things like putting the soap in the washing machine, putting toothpaste on his toothbrush, pouring milk into his cereal bowl. The extent of the "disaster" is a spill to clean. If you're stuck for ideas, just go through your daily routine in your mind. When you come to something you normally do, and it makes your gut twist a little when you think of letting your child do it, this could be just the thing. Whatever you allow him to do must feel risky for him;

and if it feels risky to you in your slightly twisted gut, it will surely feel risky to him, too. He'll think, "What if I spill the milk or mess up the washing machine?" and he'll get a little risk-rush.

The first time you offer a risky task tell him that you've noticed how much he can do and thought he might like to try some new things. The criteria to qualify a task for this stage are:

- It has no more than three steps

- He has watched you do it dozens of times

- It involves a degree of risk (like a spill or a mess), like a cracked egg

- The disaster is small, harmless and easily remedied

- You are ready to accept the outcome of his attempt, regardless of what that outcome is

First, briefly explain the task and ask if he wants to try. If he does, stand back and let him do it all by himself. It will be scary for both of you. Your reflex to stop a spill or to catch the eggshell will be strong, but you must hold yourself back. When you're tempted to stand closely by, remind yourself that it's only a small disaster and you've been smart enough to control the scope of the potential mess. Walk away and let your child try it on his own. If it's milk, you have only given him a small amount to pour anyway; it will be ok, spill or no spill. Acknowledge his anxiety because, even if he shows none at all, it's there. If he spills the milk it's simple to hand him a paper towel and then congratulate him on getting some in the bowl. Let him wipe up the rest on his own. Hand him the reins and tell him he has good judgment, and if there is a spill it'll just get cleaned up. "You're going to do great, no matter what."

> *A good scare is worth more to a man than good advice.*
> —Edgar Watson Howe

Walking away will feel weird-scary to you and exhilarating-scary to him. He may spill the milk some, but that's expected, right? I mean, isn't that the reason you haven't allowed him to do it before? The point of the exercise is for him to practice being in control and feeling at ease with making a mistake while he figures it out. When you react to the spill

> *In great attempts, it is glorious to even fail.*
> —Longinus, 1st Century A.D.

with support for his efforts, and don't step in to clean it up, his thinking will shift a bit and open up to new possibilities. Here are a few ideas for small things you can allow your child to try. Of course, adjust them to suit the age of your child:

- Pouring drinks

- Opening mail

- Toasting bread

- Cracking eggs

- Measuring baking ingredients

- Pouring soap into the clothes washer/dishwasher

- Lighting a candle (if the child is old enough)

- Putting food into the microwave

It's important that you take this step only when you are ready to let go. If your twisted gut is really strong when you think of him cracking eggs, it may be that you're not ready to allow him to do it. It's critical that you're able to accept whatever happens with a positive and empowering response. If an eggshell in the batter, or an entire egg on the floor, makes you cringe too much, don't offer that task as a choice. Maybe allowing him to measure the flour and add it to the bowl is easier for you. It's all the same to him: a new task with potential for disaster that he will try on his own. Be sure to really think through disaster-control in advance. Ask yourself the worst-case scenario and mitigate it. For example, lighting a candle poses a few potential risks that can be mitigated by confining the task to the kitchen near the sink and having a cup of water ready to extinguish the match after the candle is lit. Wiping up messes and spills only requires having paper towels nearby.

> *Bad times have a scientific value ... We learn geology the morning after an earthquake.*
> *–Ralph Waldo Emerson*

Plan the timing of the risky new task well. Make sure you have the time to be patient as he attempts new things. He'll either go too fast or too slow for your comfort level and he might ask lots of questions. For the candle task, have plenty of matches ready so he knows he can try over and over until he gets it right. If you were baking, for instance, you wouldn't want to time it right before company is expected. Your anxiety about the messy kitchen or being late with the goodies would translate to him as being anxious about his abilities to perform the task. It's great to plan to bake something to serve to your guests, but do the baking well in advance.

ONE WEEK OUT

When you see the buds of responsibility starting to show in your child, you're one week away from rolling out the Morning Peacemaker. The week before rollout you will start to concentrate your focus on the morning tasks you anticipate for the task list. By now you have been watching the morning with a different perspective and have a good idea how things are

> *Life appears to me too short to be spent in nursing animosity or registering wrongs.*
> *–Charlotte Bronte*

going; where he is having the most trouble; which tasks are difficult or simply get put off until the eleventh hour, making it frantic right before you leave in the morning. As you notice those tasks during this week, start to monitor your feelings as well. Do you get anxious if he doesn't perform tasks in the sequence you think is best? Do you find yourself hovering if he doesn't begin moving in the right direction after you nudge him with a reminder? For example, after you tell your child to put his PJs away, are you annoyed if he doesn't hop up and do it right then or if he makes his bed first? Watching the morning activities with nonjudgmental awareness will help you better understand your feelings and the possible reasons for them, and it will give you valuable practice at looking at things objectively. Just like preplanning the disaster control of the risk-rush tasks, ask yourself what the worst-case scenario will be if he does things his way? It might make more sense to you that he brushes his hair after he puts his shirt on, but does it really matter that much if he brushes his hair before? Even brushing his teeth before he eats breakfast isn't that terrible. Ok, if you happen to be a dentist and cringed just now, I offer my apology; I know I've just contradicted recommended dental hygiene protocol, but right now we are focusing on just getting the teeth brushed without reminding him. Eventually he will understand that brushing after the meal is the better way and he will make the change. What's important for you to focus on during this week is:

1. Figure out what is happening now.

2. Understand how it makes you feel, with nonjudgmental awareness.

3. Look at everything objectively and with a fresh eye.

4. Ask yourself worst-case scenario questions.

As you watch the mornings with objective purpose you might find a task that makes you really uncomfortable for this program; the thought of allowing your child control over it makes your gut twist too much. Looking at it objectively with a fresh eye may ease your initial anxiety; but if that still doesn't resolve your feelings, mitigating the worst-case scenario might do the trick. If you're still uncomfortable allowing your child to undertake that particular task on his own, consider taking it out of play for the morning.

An example might be taking vitamins. You may feel uncomfortable simply laying vitamins out and allowing your child to decide whether or not to take them. Your unwillingness may stem from the stubborn position you've taken after many morning battles. Recognizing this may ease your feelings. Maybe by looking objectively at his reluctance you'll see it as a response to the taste of the vitamin and not really defiance. But that still doesn't ease your overly twisted gut.

> *The harder you fight to hold onto specific assumptions, the more likely there's gold in letting go of them. –John Seely Brown*

The worst-case scenario is that he doesn't take his vitamins regularly. Can you mitigate things by switching to another vitamin that tastes better? If all your efforts leave you still feeling uncomfortable, consider having him take his vitamins at lunch or dinner or before the timers are set in the morning.

If, however, you find that your child's reluctance to take his vitamins is, in truth, an act of defiance, you still have options. One is to simply move vitamin-taking to another time of day or, even better, compromise. His act of defiance may be the result of his old programming or feelings of disempowerment in other areas of his life. He may see vitamins as a place to exert some control. Pushing your buttons by being reluctant to take vitamins may be his way of reestablishing some feeling of power. So think of ways you might be able to compromise to give him some control. One day, before you even take the vitamins out, ask him if he wants to take them today. If he says "No," say "OK" and see what happens. You could take him to the vitamin store so that he can pick a vitamin he thinks would be easier to take. Even if you think the vitamins he's offered now taste fine, the defiance issue will be mitigated somewhat by allowing him control over which one he chooses.

During this week it's important to see things as they are without the screen of emotion, and to look at objective solutions to problems. Doing this now will prepare your thinking so that you can compromise more easily later on. Also, any task that is essential, such as taking prescription medicine, should not be part of the Morning Peacemaker task list. Only tasks that can be done at another time of day without harm should be included.

"D" DAY

The day you plan to meet with your child is finally here. Congratulations! You've set the stage and created the perfect conditions. Now it's time to think about the timing and environment of the meeting itself.

FIFTEEN TO THIRTY

You'll need enough time to get your message across and to agree to the parameters of the program, but not so much time that it will feel overwhelming; sometime between fifteen and thirty minutes should do. Any less than fifteen and you've probably rushed and haven't given the program enough fanfare for him to take it seriously.

> *The most exquisite folly is made of wisdom spun too fine.   –Benjamin Franklin*

If you go past thirty it might mean you've gotten too detailed and made him feel overwhelmed by the complexity. Don't worry if you can't hit everything fully in the first meeting. You're in this for the long haul and there will be plenty of time to work out the kinks. Some of those kinks need to be worked out in the trenches anyway. Go through what you can and agree to talk more the following week. You will have a grace period of a few weeks in which everyone practices and nothing counts just for this purpose.

If you have an older child, he might be a bit reluctant to come to the meeting. His reluctance could be some old programming that needs replacing, so make it easy for him by guaranteeing the time maximum and setting a timer.

Plan the meeting for sometime after lunch, but not too close to dinner since it can be difficult to concentrate when everyone is hungry. Make sure your meeting isn't going to conflict with something else your child wants to do, like playing with a friend or karate class. Even if you know that your meeting will be thirty minutes maximum, he will be anxious if you want to start something too close to his other activity.

FIDDLING AND FOCUSED

It's probably unreasonable to expect a very young child to give you his undivided attention while sitting in a stiff chair as you roll out the Morning Peacemaker. He will need something to occupy his fingers so he can rally enough attention to make the meeting successful. Have a mindless activity ready and waiting at the table. Puzzles, Legos, coloring books or small action figures are great ideas. Anything that is small, uncomplicated and makes no noise will give him something to fiddle with.

> *You cannot change your destination overnight, but you can change your direction overnight. –Jim Rohn*

Have refreshments ready, too. Have you ever noticed that most of the popular children's stories include snacks? One of my favorite children's authors is Cynthia Rylant; *Henry and Mudge* and *Mr. Putter and Tabby* are just two of her popular book series that captured my boys' attention to the point that they often slept through the night holding one of her books. Her characters connected with them in many ways, but one was through their snacks. It wasn't just the snacking that made her characters and stories so beloved, but it was a factor because a good, tasty snack is a common denominator. Sharing food connects people; so provide a treat that your child doesn't get to have very often. This marks the meeting as a special event, and sharing a treat together will connect the two of you. The focus should not be on the treat for too long, though, so make the portion small and try to select something with the least amount of sugar.

PULL THE PLUG

Start the day happy and make the morning easy. Play with your child and avoid the TV. Several studies confirm that parts of the brain actually turn off when the TV is turned on. The left side of your brain that, among other things, is your logic filter, is off during TV watching. This leaves the right side of your brain soaking everything up without question, and storing it as gospel. To make matters worse, there is a change in your brain-wave pattern, too. We have four wave patterns (or activity patterns) in our brains: beta, alpha, theta and delta. Beta wave activity is our most common operating pattern. We are in beta when we read, play and talk with others. In the alpha activity pattern the waves are slower, making us more open to suggestions. Theta and delta are even slower waves produced by the unconscious mind during sleep. When the TV goes on, not only does the left side of your brain turn off, but brain activity slows to the alpha-wave pattern. So there he is, your child-sponge, sitting in front of the TV staring in a hypnotic trance with only half his brain working. In this mesmerized state, with the logic and critical thinking filters off, everything is soaked up by his unconscious mind. You might think this great if all you present to him is educational programming; but more than likely it isn't, because even the commercials are being absorbed.

Many trusted researchers and institutions are very clear now about the adverse effects TV has on us all, but on children in particular. In fact, the American Academy of Pediatrics recommends that kids under two not watch *any* TV—pause a moment, Yes that means *zero* TV—and that those older than two watch no more than *one to two hours a day* of quality programming. Though the word "quality" was not defined in the statement, I'm guessing Rugrats wouldn't qualify. So great are the threats perceived by the broadcast authority in France that it has banned channels from airing TV shows aimed at children under three.

These are bold moves based on scientific research. Even if you disagree with the strictness of the actions, you have to agree that research must have uncovered some pretty powerful negative effects. I'm sure the entertainment industry worked hard to minimize the publicity of the scientific findings and probably lobbied to squelch the restrictions and recommendations. For these institutions to do so anyway speaks volumes to me, and I hope to you as well.

In another study, researchers Robert Kubey, a professor at Rutgers University and director of the Center for Media Studies, and Mihaly Csikszentmihalyi, Professor of Psychology at Claremont Graduate University, surveyed people's reactions to television during their normal course of life. In the article "Television Addiction Is No Mere Metaphor," published in the February 2002 issue of *Scientific American*, they reported that most people described feelings of passivity and lowered alertness while watching TV. Survey participants commonly reflected that television had somehow absorbed or sucked out their energy, leaving them depleted. They said they had more difficulty concentrating after viewing than before and that their mood was about the same or worse than before. In contrast, the participants rarely indicated such difficulty after reading and reported mood improvements after playing sports or engaging in hobbies.

As you may have gathered I have a lot of strong opinions about TV watching in general. I have all but eliminated it in my life and limit the time my boys spend staring at it, though I am open-minded and flexible when we discuss it. Based on the data, I strongly recommend you unplug the TV the morning of your meeting. It'll be almost impossible for your child to reactivate his thinking brain right after having it turned off while watching the TV. However, if limiting the screen time will create a big conflict, get it in early and turn it off well in advance of the meeting. He should be plugged in to you and to himself, not the TV, when you come together.

A Picture is Worth a Thousand Words

Since we all think in pictures, visual aids are important. You'll need to be able to show your child what you're talking about. Along with the analog clock and timers, have a few examples of the calendar page ready so he understands how simple it is. Because you won't have agreement on the actual list of tasks when you prepare the examples, take this opportunity to lighten up the meeting with humor. Instead of guessing at the tasks to which you'll eventually

> *A sense of humor is part of the art of leadership, of getting along with people, of getting things done.*
> *–Dwight D. Eisenhower*

agree, make up some silly ones like *eat candy, annoy sister* and, for budding astronauts, *fly to the moon and back*. That'll get his attention and make him happy. Let him go off on a short tangent about all the other fun and silly tasks he would like to add to the page. It'll lighten the meeting and it might encourage him to create a page design of his own, so have some supplies ready. It'll be interesting for you to see what he thinks and it will be empowering for him to create his page. With the computer instruction included later in the book, you'll be able to come pretty close to creating whatever he dreams up.

If your child doesn't want to design something, that's ok too because just picking the format he likes from your samples will create ownership feelings. At subsequent meetings revisit the page design issue. As I discussed

> *If I could tell you what it meant, there would be no point in dancing it.*
> *–Isodora Duncan*

earlier, neither of you will know what works best for him visually until he uses the page for a while. He might be more willing to offer creative input after he has had a chance to work with the first design for a few weeks. Keep in mind that everything is open for discussion and revision at any meeting. You can try it and change it, and try it and change it, until it feels just right for both of you.

It's important to point out that his calendar page is for him alone. It should not only reflect his likes and promote him personally, it is also for him to mark as part of the morning. Your handwriting should not be visible on the page because, during the morning, *he* is in charge of his tasks; it is an opportunity for him to practice self-evaluation. If you mark the page for him or correct something he wrote, you will be taking a piece of the ownership and it will be counterproductive. Only his touch should ever be seen on the page.

You'll already have prepared the analog clock, with multi-colored time slice segments, and labeled the multi-use timers. Though you'll have an idea of the right amount of time for each segment on the clock and snooze settings from your earlier work in Chapter Four, be flexible about making any changes that result from your discussion. You might have prepared the clock with ten-minute time slices and

> *Success is a science; if you have the conditions, you get the result.   –Oscar Wilde*

need to change to five-minute slices. It's easy to simply divide the time up a bit more on the clock face and reset the timers. Expanding the slices from five to ten minutes is easy, too. Just outline pairs of five-minute slices with a bright color and lightly shade across the top of them with the same outline color. Don't completely cover the original colors of each slice, so your child can benefit from the extra data. Creating the clock is pretty simple but, if you prefer, I have two versions of the clock available for purchase on the website, *www.Peacemaker-Coach.com*. Remember, the materials you prepare for the meeting will be created using your new thinking and, therefore, will be the empowering tools your child will really use to accomplish this bit of learning. You will be amazed and dazzled by the results. The greater the effort before the meeting, the greater the meeting will be.

CHAPTER SEVEN

Finally Meeting Face to Face

A leader is best when people barely know he exists. When his work is done, his aim fulfilled, they will say: We did it ourselves.

–Lao Tzu

Once you and your child are at the table, you have the fiddle things, a snack, your outline and all the visual aids, your first sentence needs to be straightforward and empowering. Here's an example:

"I've noticed a good change in you and it's gotten me thinking that you're growing up and that you're ready to try doing some things on your own. What do you think?"

It's that simple. If you're stuck finding just the right thing to say, you can use these words. They will work equally well, whether your child is two-years old and you're going to put two tasks on his list or nine-years old and he'll have seven tasks. Your recognition of his growth and your empowerment will be a message universally

> *I believe in the discipline of silence and could talk about it for hours.*
> *–George Bernard Shaw*

well received. Ending your opening comments by asking him what he thinks will get him talking because he'll want to tell you even more about how he has changed and grown up. Stay quiet, attentive and positive to encourage even more talking. It might be that telling you about his growth will be the first time he's actually put coherent thoughts behind the feelings he's surely been having. He is likely to have a lot to say, so let him. It will help to sort him out and calm him down.

It's critical that he talk to you. You will get nowhere unless there is an open dialog. A major factor encouraging participation is trust. He must trust that you will really listen and that you will honestly consider his ideas. If you have a hidden agenda he will surely sense it, even if you paste a

> *It is the responsibility of leadership to provide opportunity, and the responsibility of individuals to contribute. –William Pollard*

smile on your face; so either bring it out or lose it. Everything you do from this point on must be open and honest; all cards are played face up. Trust is built by matching your actions to your words. Right now, pay attention with sincerity. You don't have to agree with everything he says, as long as you respect his view, allow it to flow uninterrupted and consider it honestly.

As he talks, use your outline to take notes. Not only will this ensure you have everything remembered correctly later, it will also demonstrate to him that you consider his thoughts important enough to write them down. Your pre-planning and attention to detail will impress him and impress upon him that he is being given a real chance to practice being responsible.

From here the meeting will flow in a general direction through your outline. There will surely be a few deviations, as one thought leads him into a connected thought outside the scope of the meeting. Allow these deviations with an open mind, but watch for an opening to steer the conversation gently back to the points on your outline. If the meeting veers too far left or right he will be confused later. Go slowly and enjoy the scenery, but stay on the right road.

THE TASKS

Since you've done so much thinking about this already you've eliminated the complicated tasks and simplified the rest. You've anticipated his thoughts and you've spent weeks watching with objectivity, so there will be many wonderful thoughts, observations and feelings you'll want to share with

> *Are you really listening ... or are you just waiting for your turn to talk? –Robert Montgomery*

your child right then and there. But you aren't going to—at least not right now, and certainly not all at once. It's time to let him do most of the talking by simply asking him to tell you what he thinks his chores should be in the morning. Stay as quiet as you can and allow some pauses in the conversation. Though you've been thinking about this a while, it's the first time he has heard anything about it and he'll need time to think. If he gets really stuck or talks too far off topic, give him an example of a task or two that you do, or ask questions about his morning that day or the day before.

It's likely that he will task himself with more than you think, loading up on tasks from all times of the day. It may be a sign he doesn't understand how to prioritize his morning, or it's to impress you with how much he knows and thinks he can do. Write all his tasks down—everything, even the ones that don't apply to the morning or that are new tasks he's dreamed up. He may even throw in entertainment "tasks" like watching TV or playing video games. Maybe he's testing the parameters of the program, or maybe he is in a routine of watching TV or playing video games in the morning and has confused the habit with a task. Whatever he suggests doesn't matter; write them all down and try not to comment just yet. After he presents his ideas, discuss each one to hone the list. As both of you remove tasks from the morning he'll see his burdens becoming less and less, he'll see the priorities emerge and he'll be able to separate habits from tasks. Perhaps the difficulty you've been having in the morning stems from his unconscious belief that the morning was too filled with work. As you whittle the list to a few simple tasks you'll demonstrate how much easier the morning really is. Things like feeding the hamster, tidying up his room, homework, practicing a musical instrument or sport can come off the morning list, though they still get done each day. It's just that the morning will be a special block of time in which he is in charge of a few particular tasks. It's the practice period of the day. Once this special block of time ends each day, everything returns to normal, including his need to contribute to the family by doing his other chores. You will be building a positive attitude about the morning with his special empowerment over really easy and standard things. Pointing out the small number of tasks will relax him right then and there.

> *Leadership is getting someone to do what they don't want to do, to achieve what they want to achieve. –Tom Landry*

Another very important point to bring up at the meeting is that he will be the one to decide the order in which tasks are completed each morning. He may feel a better rhythm in making his bed before he gets dressed, or he may like to brush his hair and teeth before he comes to breakfast. The order doesn't matter, as long as it all gets done. You can list them on his calendar page in any order he tells you, but be sure to empower him with the flexibility to mix it up at any time on any day. If he misses a task in the morning, it still doesn't really matter, because he'll just do whatever he missed later that day. Easy, no pain, no punishment, no nag, no disappointed looks from you—he just tries and keeps on trying. As we will see later, lessons learned when a task is missed can be very effective.

Visual Aids

Training Wheel #1—The Calendar Page

When you introduce the calendar page, tell your child that you understand it might be tough at first being responsible for his tasks in the morning, so you have a helper for him. When you show him one of the examples you prepared in advance, his picture will surely catch his attention. The first image you choose should be fairly recent and a special shared memory. Take a minute to remember it together. He is the star, and being right smack dab in the middle of the page is a big ego boost. You'll explain that every day he will have a page like this that he can use to help him remember what he needs to do. Each day there will be a different picture of him or of something he likes, to make him feel good as he starts his day.

Point out how the tasks are arranged on the page and giggle with him at the silly tasks you listed. Show him the check-off boxes for his mark as he completes things, so that he can keep track of what he has done and what's left to do. Tell him that he is the only one who will be allowed to write on his calendar page. Point out the times at the top corners of the page, along with the day and the date. While he's looking at it, ask a few questions:

- I like having your picture on the page. How about you?

- Where do you think the tasks should be on the page?

- Do you think the tasks should be listed in a special order?

- Do you like the way I arranged the page?

- If you were going to make a calendar page, what would it look like? Would you draw it for me?

If he wants to design something, he can either start from scratch or he can mark up any of your examples. Praise and love whatever he designs, even if it's silly or you think it's impossible to recreate on your computer. Don't worry about your computer ability. As I said earlier, with the instructions later in the book, you'll be able to do almost anything he comes up with. Tell him you'll try your best to copy his design and that you're so happy you asked for his ideas. If it looks like he'll be drawing for more than five minutes or so, you'll have to steer him back to the conversation gently so he isn't completely sidetracked,

> *The art of teaching is the art of assisting discovery.*
> *–Mark Van Doren*

forgetting the whole point of the exercise. Assure him that he can work on his design as long as he likes later and that you'll do everything you can to duplicate his masterpiece, no matter when he gives it to you. If he doesn't want to sketch anything just let him pick from the design options you have ready and ask if he likes the orientation of the tasks. Make any changes he wants to the page, remembering it is *his* page and it must be a reflection of his tastes, not yours. Make notes on the sample page he chooses so you're sure you have understood his comments, and let him give you the final approval.

TRAINING WHEEL #2—THE MORNING PEACEMAKER CLOCK

Before you unveil the clock ask him to think about how long it takes to do each task. Discuss the tasks briefly and then bring out the clock you have prepared with pie slice segments and explain why you sliced it. As you go through each task, write his time estimates down and track them on the clock with skinny post-it notes labeled with the task.

> *Never look back unless you're planning to go that way.*
> *–Henry David Thoreau*

For example, your child estimates it will take him five minutes to make his bed. Put a post-it labeled "bed" on the clock at the five-minute mark. If he estimates another five minutes to get dressed, put the "dress" post-it at the ten-minute mark, five minutes after the last task. Continue through all the tasks like this until you have the total amount of time he estimates he'll need to do everything on the list. He will most likely tell you everything is easy—five minutes or less! Resist the temptation to ask him why, then, everything has taken forever and needed your constant *nagging* for it to even get done at all!

Breathe deeply and let the experiences of the past become a source of strength to keep you on track with the present and future. You are in the process of fixing the problems. Regardless of what you know to be more reasonable estimates of time, put his ideas on the clock and write them down. Contradicting him right now will only make him defensive and feel he already has it wrong. Prepare him for later compromise by talking about how our bodies work in the morning. Explain that there is a transition time everyone goes through to get from the complete rest of sleep to the activity of the morning. Because everything seems to take more time in the morning, tell him that you often get up a bit early just so you can enjoy the transition and not feel rushed.

Here are some interesting facts about the sleep–wake transition. Your body's clock is a collection of nerve cells in the hypothalamus, a gland located just above the brain stem. These cells regulate the release of hormones that prepare us for rest and activity. Studies conducted on adults show a sharp increase in hormone activity within the first hour of waking, with the highest increase seen fifteen to thirty minutes afterwards. What this means is that your body chemistry goes through a transition, and it can take some time before all systems are online. Explaining to your child that you allow extra time for yourself because it helps you start each day relaxed and happy will help him understand and recognize his own sleep–wake transition as well. I wouldn't go into the details, but knowing this for yourself may make understanding your child's morning start-up routine easier.

After you've gone through each task, ask him what time he thinks the morning at home ends. This will be whatever time you and he need to be out the door in the morning. He may not know the exact time, but he'll be able to tell you that the morning at home ends when he has to leave to go to school, for example. If you don't leave home early in the morning, come to an agreement about the time the morning ends, using another event or benchmark, like the time you go to the park or library.

The end of the morning will be the time that morning tasks need to be completed. When we began this program in my home, both boys were on the same elementary school schedule, so the end of our morning was 8:30 during the week. It's easy and natural to expect all the morning tasks to be done by 8:30. On Saturday and Sunday, however, there are no regular early morning departure requirements, though we all agreed that the morning chores still needed to be done. Before we decided on the right time to end a weekend morning, we talked about the need to have a break from the fast pace of the work week. We all felt the need to laze about and go slow after a week full of tight time schedules. The right end-of-morning time for us on the weekend is 10:00. On a side note, establishing the morning's end on the weekend has had the side benefit of helping our family get activities started. Before the Morning Peacemaker, my boys floated around without direction. Breakfast turned into brunch and they often felt as though they had wasted a big part of the day. Now we have the sensation of freedom from a tight morning schedule while still having enough time to make the most of the day. A plan is important everyday, but be flexible when you can be. I'll also point out that, when Michael became a middle schooler, his schedule changed. His mornings now end at 7:40 while Jack's have remained 8:30. The transition was easy because each boy has his own set of timers.

It may not be necessary, or even wise, to change the time parameters for the weekend or according to a fluctuation in weekday morning schedules. Consistency is very important for good habits to form, so try to keep everything the same everyday as much as possible for the first few months. Once you decide the issue, put a post-it labeled "all done" on the clock.

WHEN DO WE START?

Your child now knows how long tasks will take (well, his estimates anyway), and knows when the morning ends. Now ask him when it should begin. At this point he may recognize the cluster of task post-its showing his speedy time estimates and the larger amount of "extra" time available before the morning ends. Now is the time to suggest spreading things out and allowing a little extra time for tasks.

I recommended dividing the time on the clock into pie-slice segments according to the number of tasks on his list. For one to four tasks, the clock is colored in five-minute slices, up to half an hour (six slices), and for five to eight tasks, segments are in ten-minute slices for one hour (or another six slices). To help him reach a reasonable starting time, suggest backing into the start according to your pie-slice segments on the clock rather than basing the starting time solely on how long he thinks he can complete his tasks. Suggest your child use the full block of time, sixty minutes or thirty minutes, so that the official start of the morning is an hour or half an hour before you leave the house. Here is an example:

Jack leaves for school at 8:30. He has seven tasks and estimated time as follows:

1. Bed—2 minutes

2. Dressed—2 minutes

3. PJs—1 minute

4. Teeth—2 minutes

5. Hair—1 minute

6. Breakfast—3 minutes

7. Backpack—2 minutes

Jack estimates thirteen minutes to complete them all. The clock is sliced into ten-minute segments and has eight post-its: seven tasks taking his estimated thirteen minutes and the post-it marking the time his morning ends—8:30.

If your child's clock resembles Jack's, suggest that, rather than crowding his morning all together in thirteen minutes, he allow an hour—all six slices—for everything. Explain that this may be much more time than he needs but it will give him a little buffer, just in case he gets distracted one day. Remind him that, if he zips through his tasks just like he thinks he will, the rest of the time is free and easy.

Explain that the beginning time is the official start each day and signals his freedom to do his chores as he see fit, and that you aren't going to remind or nag him. Let him know that, if he decides to start early, that's ok too. Make sure he understands that you are, and always will be, there to help him; the only difference now is that it will be for him to decide what he needs help with and when to ask for it. Tell him that you might have been stepping in too soon before and that you want to give him the chance to do things on his own until he is ready for help.

If your child reacts excitedly and says he's all set to go, just move on to the timers; however, if he seems reluctant or hesitant, it could be that he just needs a minute to incorporate the change in responsibility and start the reprogramming process in his mind. If it's more than that and he seems doubtful of his readiness or abilities, go back over the tasks and ask him which one makes him nervous. Help him to think objectively through the tasks by looking at each one again.

After you've eliminated the tasks themselves as the source of his fear, but he is still doubtful, ask him what he thinks the morning will be like with this new way of doing things. He might be envisioning a morning in which you are unavailable, distant or unloving; he may think he will be abandoned. You can overcome this by telling him how you see the morning with this new program. Tell him you see it even more loving and happy because there will be peace and trust rather than nagging. Reassure him that you'll always be there to help and, now that he has both you and his calendar page, days will be brighter.

He may be swirling with the negative thoughts of failure left over from past experience. Encourage him to ask you any "what if" questions he has: "What if I can't get the cap off the toothpaste?" "What if I can't find my clothes?" "What if I can't get my shirt buttoned?" "What if I lose track of time?" "What if I'm late?" "What if I don't get everything done in time?" If he can't articulate his feelings of dread, pose a few of these for him and answer them this way:

"I expect you to need help and to make mistakes. Everyone makes mistakes or gets new things wrong in the beginning. I've been doing this a long time now and I still make mistakes and forget to do things. Of course it happens. Just ask me and I'll be happy to help. It's my job to help you— and I love my job. All learning takes time and practice, just like the time and practice it took for you to learn to drink from a cup or ride your bike. I helped you while you practiced, but you were the one who did it in the end. I'm here to help you just like that now, and I'll always be here to help you whenever you need me. If you didn't make mistakes I would think something was wrong."

I would say that 99% of the children would be able to move on from here. If yours are in the 1% group, don't lose faith. Go back to the tasks and take half of them off the list. Tell him you want him to believe in himself as much as you believe in him, and to build his confidence he can start out with half of the tasks and even pick which ones he feels most confident about. The other tasks still need to be done, but those tasks just won't be part of the special practice time until he is ready.

After your child sees he can do these first few tasks easily, you'll add the others at a pace comfortable to him. The main thing is to get him started on the right foot, even if it is only with one task. Eventually, your child will end up in the right place, so just get him going. Allow him to decide his starting point, and be just as excited by a list with only one task as you would by a list of seven.

TRAINING WHEEL #3—THE SNOOZE TIMERS

If, during your discussion about the timing for the morning tasks, your child expressed anxiety about losing track of time, you have the perfect way to introduce the timers. Put them on the table and let him have one to hold while you use the other to explain how they work. Tell him the timers are his snooze buttons, just like the ones on alarm clocks. They are his tools to help him keep track of time in the morning.

Each snooze segment is labeled in order from one to six, and each snooze segment lasts either five or ten minutes. When ten minutes have passed, the timer will go off to alert him. When one snooze goes off, the remaining snoozes are automatically keeping track of time and will go off every ten minutes until all six snoozes, or all sixty minutes, have passed. As he presses the button to turn off a snooze alarm, say snooze #1, he knows that the first ten minutes have passed and that he is starting snooze #2. That means he has five snoozes left in which to finish his task list. The snooze alarms are his personal assistants helping him to be successful.

Both the snooze timers and clock are available for purchase on the website, *www.Peacemaker-Coach.com*. The timers track up to three separate events, with easy-to-read and -use buttons. Any multi-use timer will do. I don't recommend a single-function timer because it will require your assistance to reset continually for the next snooze interval. More than two timers are cumbersome to handle also, so stick with a multi-function timer that allows for three timed events.

USING THE CLOCK AND CALENDAR TOGETHER

At this point in the meeting you'll connect the use of all his tools so that he will understand how each one supports him as he practices being responsible in the morning. The best way to do this is to walk him through hypothetical use. After a bit of time playing with his timers you'll bring out again the clock and the calendar page your child likes. Review briefly how each tool works and then tie their functions together. The calendar page helps keep track of the tasks he needs to do. He checks off the box for "make bed" when he completes that task so he knows which tasks are left to do. The colorful clock helps him plan his time in smaller slices and the timers guarantee any distraction won't last more than five or ten minutes.

Tell him that, when all the tasks are completed and the calendar page is marked off, he'll put the page and his timers in the bin or drawer, wherever you agree these things should go. If he finishes everything on the list early, GREAT! Put the page in the bin, but keep the timers. Tell him that his timers will still help him keep track of time so that he's ready when it's time to leave for the day. When the last snooze goes off he will put them in the bin with his calendar page right before he puts his shoes on. Simple and sweet! He will relax, having had a practice run in his mind.

THE GRACE PERIOD

I allowed my boys an entire month for the grace period. This meant that they were guaranteed their full allowance while they practiced, even if they missed a task or two. After the month of grace everything counted toward incentive pay, but I still allowed them to fix chores they missed. Gradually tasks were taken off the "fix list," which meant they could not be corrected in the morning. For example, if they had forgotten to make their beds, I wouldn't allow them to make their beds until they came home from school. When they came home, the first thing they had to do was to make their beds. In the event they had forgotten to brush their teeth in the early stages, I would allow them to dash quickly and fix that problem. As I said, we gradually moved, task by task, to the point at which none of the tasks could be fixed until later in the day—even teeth, breakfast and a packed backpack.

Don't mention this at your first meeting. When the time comes that they are completely accountable for their tasks, enough practice will have taken place and it will feel natural. Telling all this now will only scare them needlessly.

INCENTIVES

Depending upon the age of your child it may not be necessary to have this discussion at the first meeting. For children under five or those who have responded enthusiastically to the new plan, you could skip it; although, if you're already giving an allowance of some kind, you could take this opportunity to tie them together. If you elect to defer the incentive discussion, simply reach an agreement about how long the grace period should be once you begin this program, and move on to how you will have review meetings.

In the event you need to help your child accept his new responsibilities, open the discussion with a question very similar to the one with which you started the meeting:

> "As I noticed the good changes in you, I started thinking that we should talk about your allowance. Now that you'll be responsible for your mornings, it seems like the perfect time to tie them together. What do you think?"

Whether you have been giving an allowance or not, the question is the same. I use the word "allowance" to mean any reward for tasks completed, not just money. If you give your child a certain amount of TV/screen time, or visits to the park or zoo, these can be considered "allowances," too.

Earlier we discussed money incentives. I hope by now it is obvious that money is just a tool that everyone uses to get more of what they want. If you believe that money is the right incentive, be glad that you have something that will motivate your child. It took some time for me to understand this concept, but once I got over my hang-up about money incentives, I offered it in the same way a salesman gets paid: a base guaranteed salary with a commission bonus tied to every sale. Applying this to our morning program meant that, at the end of each week, my boys were guaranteed a base dollar amount, regardless of their success in managing their morning tasks during the week.

As an incentive to be successful, they would receive an extra bonus amount for every successfully managed morning. I arrived at the base/bonus split by looking at their current allowance amounts. I made sure the base was slightly more than half of their current allowance and that the daily bonus, when added to the base for seven successful mornings, would give them the potential to earn more than their current allowance.

For example, at age ten Michael received $8.00 each week in allowance. With the new base/bonus plan his base went to $4.50 guaranteed with an extra $1.00 for each successful morning. He now had the earning potential of $11.50—that is, $3.50 more than his current allowance! After our first month using the program, I offered a choice between the base/bonus scenario and their current flat-rate allowance amount; I would either pay out the allowance or the base/bonus at the end of every week.

My willingness to guarantee reward caught them off guard. They were a bit skeptical and asked many questions to find the loophole they just knew had to be there. With each "what if" scenario they presented, I was given insight as to their thoughts, fears and intentions. Each time, my answer was the same—that I would, in fact, pay the base and earned bonus—they relaxed a bit more and began to trust my intentions.

My younger son jumped at the base/bonus option right away. It is his nature to always think the best possible scenario will happen and he is more confident with new things, so he was able to visualize great potential. Michael, however, is not as confident and wasn't comfortable with the risk of losing his guaranteed amount,

> *Motivation is what gets you started. Habit is what keeps you going.*   *–Jim Rohn*

even though it was less than he now had the opportunity to earn. So I told him that, during each weekly review he would have a chance to change his mind, but until then he would receive his regular $8.00 allowance guaranteed.

After two weeks he switched over to the base/bonus plan. He watched his brother raking in the dough and realized his own lost income because he saw how easy it was to be successful in the morning. Each week they have the same option to switch back to straight salary, but neither of them even considers it now. By the way, I hope you caught the shift in Michael's self-confidence. He saw proof positive that he was capable and, therefore, opened up to the risk. Yippie!

When you have the initial discussion about incentives, your child is likely to have a lot of ideas—some outrageous and some reasonable. Be passive in

> *Always bear in mind that your own resolution to succeed is more important than any one thing.*
> –Abraham Lincoln

your reaction to whatever he spouts out. He is probably experiencing the feeling of sanctioned power for the first time and may try flexing his new muscles. Just as a pendulum swings way out from the left to way out to the right, it's normal that your child may have some overly enthusiastic ideas. Your initial reaction may be to think he is greedy if he asks for the outrageous. He isn't greedy; he's normal. First, it's a normal developmental stage for children under thirteen to be self-centered. During this stage in development it's appropriate for his focus to be on himself and how things affect him, to the exclusion of others. As he gets closer to the next developmental stage, one in which he becomes group-centered, his self-centered focus softens and he begins to include the effects on others more and more.

> *Children and zip fasteners do not respond to force.*
> –Katharine Whitehorn

Second, try to remember that a child of five (or even ten) has no real understanding of how hard it is to earn money, or even how much money is reasonable for a kid of that age to have. He won't—can't—understand the economics of your budget, no matter how you try to explain it to him. You might tell him that from the money you earn all the bills, groceries, clothes, college savings, etc., must be paid for, but it won't connect with him. He may think about your story and logically understand the basics, but he won't feel it personally. He may still ask for the moon and the stars, so don't be unnerved by it. Remember, you still have to agree before it is implemented, so negotiate and compromise to reach an agreement that motivates him and is still acceptable to you.

> *Precedents, once established, are so much positive power.*
> –James Madison

You may find that coming to an agreement about incentives is contentious. Perhaps it's more of the old programming in one or both of you. If it starts to go in that direction, decide to leave the resolution for the next meeting and stick with his current allowance. Reinforce that nothing can be included in the morning plan until everyone agrees. That even means that the new plan itself doesn't begin until everyone agrees. You'll just have to come together the following week and try again, though it's very unlikely you'll have much conflict.

Truly, nothing can be done until everyone agrees. You have the opportunity to build trust and confidence here. Stick to the plan and show him you are serious about compromise and agreement. Show him his important role in deciding the issues of the morning by not deciding anything, if need be. It is better for nothing to get done now rather than to have you override things with your position of authority to establish the rules. That is the basic idea James Madison and our founding fathers used to frame the most successful form of government in history. Follow their excellent example and you won't go wrong. If it takes a week or so, that's fine. I guarantee that 99.9% of children will respond, even if it takes longer for some than others.

Until Next Time

End the meeting with a quick run-down of the key points you discussed. You'll re-state the agreements and the open issues and set the time for your next meeting. Point out how fast this meeting was and tell him that the next meeting is likely to be even shorter because so much of the big stuff was discussed today. As you clean up the supplies and put things away, talk about how cool it is that he's growing up and how glad you are at the thought of him maturing. Let him see, hear and feel from you the promise of freedom and happiness that is in store for you both as he becomes more practiced at deciding things on his own. Smile, hug and allow him to go off to play quietly without the TV for a few hours so he has the opportunity to replay the conversation in his mind and think it through.

You, too, need some time to mull over the meeting. Make time to write down the insights you gained from your conversation. You may have had thoughts during the meeting to which you didn't want to call your child's attention by writing them down in front of him. You may not have had a chance to fully capture an idea because the meeting was moving along too quickly. Fill in all the gaps now and make your notes clear so you can use them to refresh your memory before the next meeting.

Your notes will also keep you objective in your attitude. If you find yourself writing words like "angry" or "greedy," these are your red flags; they indicate your thinking is emotionally based and could be part of the old programming you're in the process of changing. Step outside the emotions and stay focused.

REVIEW MEETINGS

Once the Morning Peacemaker starts, it is important that you and your child meet each week to talk about the prior week's successes and challenges. During those meetings you'll bring out the daily calendar pages for that week and allow him to look them over. No doubt he will immediately look at all his pictures and be uplifted by them again, which sets a positive tone for the meeting. Let your child tell you which picture was his favorite during the week, and tell him how much fun you had making the pages, because you love his pictures so much.

> *It's not the load that breaks you down, it is the way you carry it.*
> *–Lou Holtz*

There may be a general "How's it going?" "Fine." type dialog. You can spur deeper conversation by asking questions about what worked well and what was difficult. Start by pointing out something he is doing well, such as putting his pajamas away. Ask him what it is about this task that makes it so easy. Then ask about things that appear to be more troublesome, such as the task of marking his page and putting it in the bin. Ask him questions and point out where you usually find the page later in the day. Ask him what his strategy could be to get it in the bin. If he has an idea that sounds reasonable, let him use it. Try not to offer suggestions just yet, unless he is really stuck for a strategy. After you both agree to his idea, make sure he understands that it is his strategy to implement.

The calendar page example was an actual challenge Michael had at one time. I often found his page in the family room and his timers in the bin. During our review meetings he came up with different strategies to make it easier to remember, like putting the page in front of his bedroom door so that he would be reminded to take it with him downstairs. We talked about my limited role in implementing his strategy and that I would continue to put his page on his bedside table in the morning, leaving it up to him to put the page where he thought it would be most useful. The bottom line was that he was responsible to implement his strategies. His strategies were consistently unsuccessful. During one meeting he noticed that the timers were magnetized on the back and could stick together. He asked me to sandwich his calendar page

> *The function of leadership is to produce more leaders, not more followers.*
> *–Ralph Nader*

between his two timers so that they would all travel together and end up in the bin. Bingo! He found the right strategy and it worked great.

The point here is that, during reviews when the stress of an unsuccessful morning isn't present, Michael and I could think objectively. He came up with many ideas and implemented few. Over the course of a few weeks he began to realize

> *Give a man a fish, and you feed him for a day; teach him how to fish, and you feed him for a lifetime.*
> *–Chinese Proverb*

two key things: One, the problem wasn't going to be solved by anyone but him; and two, he was missing out on bonus pay each time he forgot to return the page to the bin.

I had also offered suggestions during this period, such as putting the page in the bin right away and marking it off from there. But my idea was only going to become a working strategy if he implemented it. He didn't like my ideas, but couldn't come up with a workable one and continued to lose bonus pay. When Michael finally came up with the calendar page sandwich strategy, it worked mainly because it was based on his personal experience and observation. Being patient is important while your child learns to solve problems for himself. I've noticed just how clever they truly are.

As the review meeting continues, point out patterns of success and challenges. Ask your child questions about his thoughts and feelings rather than his actions, such as: "Why is it hard to remember the page and not the timers?" "Why do you have trouble remembering to brush your hair?" "What do you think would make it easier to remember?" If he doesn't have a clue how to fix something, offer ideas from

> *It takes two wings to fly.*
> *–J. Kelly*

your experience. But don't lead the discussion with them; instead, offer your suggestions as a last resort, because you're trying to get him to practice solving problems on his own. If he learns how to help himself with his morning tasks he will be ready to apply the same techniques in school and college, when the going gets really rough.

During the review you also have the opportunity to talk about the way things are going from your perspective. This is your time to give him feedback and discuss how things are affecting you. The actions of one impact everyone else in the family. The Morning Peacemaker must do just that:

> *Every man's got to figure to get beat sometimes.*
> —Joe Louis

make peace for everyone or it will ultimately be good for no one. Make sure to tell him the good things and then tell him about any problems you're having. One good thing on which I used to comment was the fact that their timers helped keep me on track, too. I still benefit from them and use them for myself at other times of the day.

One problem I raised at a review meeting was that, when a snooze timer sounded, the boys were not turning it off soon enough. The ongoing sound frustrated me. I told them it brought up my nag-reflex because I was about to shout at them to turn the sound off. I asked for their help. They told me they would try to turn off the timers sooner. Though we have an occasionally long timer sound, generally it's gotten better. By giving and taking with your children you openly reinforce their importance in the family and the success of the program.

After the review meeting, take a minute to write down the net take from the discussion so you have notes for the next meeting, and then watch how the week goes. Try not to remind your child of any strategy he talked about, because reminding him to implement a strategy is just like reminding him to put on his socks. Let him have the freedom to choose his destiny.

It's important to understand the need for these weekly meetings, but I would not go into too much detail about them with your child now at the rollout meeting. Just let him know he will have an opportunity every week to add his ideas and suggest changes to the plan until everything feels just right.

Onward and Upward

You've done it! Congratulations! The ball is officially rolling now. You have work ahead of you, but it will feel different this time. As the rollout meeting ends, be excited by what's in store. Your child will grow and learn things about himself that nothing but personal experience could teach him. Learning can be tough sometimes—not only for him but for you, too. You'll encounter times that make you want to give up. But hold fast: Those are the times when breakthroughs are made. If you keep your focus on your objectives it will be easier to see those tough times as positive signs of change.

Your child is likely to test and push and test some more. He's figuring it all out the best way he can by experiencing it. Some tests may be outright defiance while others may be subtle deviations to agreements. Keep the agreed rules clear and enforced at all times during the week. Changes should only be discussed at review. You will also find it difficult to keep to the agreement at times. If he has been especially naughty one week you might think he is deserving of nothing and be tempted to withhold payout at the review. He may have gone 0 for 7 another week and you think withholding the base is a fitting consequence. Strong resolve, commitment and a focus on the long-term goals are your anchors to keep you on track. Making an executive decision to withhold payout will set you back, since it will just take longer to build up trust again.

The next chapter will outline the three phases of this program and discuss briefly some of the behaviors you may encounter, as well as solutions to help keep you anchored. You'll find insights to help you understand the cause of your child's behavior and to give you ideas for dealing with it. But don't panic: Your child won't exhibit all of the behaviors listed, nor will they occur all at once.

CHAPTER EIGHT

Bringing It All Together

If confusion is the first step to knowledge, I must be a genius.

—Larry Leisner

After our discussion of learning theories, genetics, consciousness, help-lessness, calendar pages, timers, review meetings and self confidence, you've learned quite a lot and I'm sure you've had a variety of reactions. You may have recognized some positive things you're already doing but, until now, hadn't known the science behind them. You may have recognized some things you're doing that you thought were positive, but now know better. Doesn't knowing make all the difference? As uncomfortable as it may be to recognize mistakes, it's the knowledge that will help you choose differently next time.

> *If a man who enjoys a lesser happiness beholds a greater one, let him leave aside the lesser to gain the greater.*
>
> *—Buddha*

There may have been ideas that finally came together and clicked for you; and, I'm guessing, there were ideas you wanted to reject offhand or with which you simply disagreed. I hope that you experienced all of these thoughts and feelings. Your reactions tell you a lot about where you are today. Recognizing where you are now in relation to where you want to go is the first step toward actually getting there.

Explaining each component of the Peacemaker Parent method separately should enable you to truly understand how important each piece of the puzzle is in making the whole a success. It's when you bring these pieces together in the Morning Peacemaker that you see the simplicity of the big picture. Just as in nature, this program is very efficient, as long as we understand the basics. All the theories and ideas we discussed are really supporting the same basic principle: People operate best in a positive environment.

> *Habit is habit, and not to be flung out the window by any man, but coaxed downstairs a step at a time. –Mark Twain*

Therefore, although we are all complex individuals, we operate efficiently as long we know two things: Where to find our on/off switch and how to keep ourselves fueled properly. By keeping these two simple ideas in mind, your actions will naturally follow so that your child will perform beyond your wildest dreams. Keep yourself and your child fueled with positive thoughts and a supporting environment and neither of you can miss.

WHAT DOES IT LOOK LIKE?

Some of you may be asking, "Now that I know all of this, what does it really look like? What actually happens every day? How do I put it all together and, when I do, will I be overwhelmed?" The best answer to these questions is to give you a picture of what the Morning Peacemaker looks like in action as you pass through its three phases: Initiation, Slipping/Testing and Routine.

Before describing each phase in greater detail, let's look first at the stages of learning. The first is the *unconscious incompetence* stage: We don't know that we don't know something. After an idea is introduced, we move into *conscious incompetence*, because now we

> *We cannot become what we need to be by remaining what we are. –Max DePree*

know that we don't know something. Then we become *consciously competent* by learning and practicing so that, with conscious effort, we can perform the skill. After a period of time, the once-conscious skill becomes an unconscious habit; we are now unconsciously competent, performing the skill automatically.

You might think this last stage is the finish line you're striving to cross, but it isn't. There will be mistakes that indicate a slip in competence. The mistake triggers the need for additional conscious effort for competence to return. The back-and-forth between competence and incompetence is like the swinging of a pendulum. With each cycle of swings, the distance traveled lessens until the back-and-forth quiets to a complete rest: true and consistent unconscious competence.

As you read about the three phases below, you'll see that I've included a few examples from my personal experience using this program, but by no means is this a complete list. To have included all that I want to share would require a separate book. Therefore, I've limited myself to these few. But regardless of any list I could create, there will always be more to add, because the lessons we are teaching with this program are ever evolving the behavior of our children. As children grow and become more aware, their actions will change, creating a never-ending list of situations for us to learn from.

There are many ways in which your child will respond to the changes in his idea of personal power. Each child and family is unique and will encounter and perceive situations in his own ways. The situations you encounter are not only for you to learn from; they can be of great learning benefit for all of us. To share your information with the rest of us could be the greatest gift. I encourage you to add your own experiences to this list. Help and be helped in the company of like-minded Peacemaker Parents who share a common passion and purpose, because sharing makes the difference between individual success and promoting greatness for us all. You'll find an ever-growing community at *www.Peacemaker-Coach.com*.

INITIATION PHASE

Your child begins the Morning Peacemaker unconsciously incompetent; he doesn't know that he has any power to control his results in the morning. He quickly moves into conscious incompetence as you roll out the program during the initial meeting. From the very first day using the program through roughly the second month, you and your child will be working to build conscious competence. Your preparation for the program means that you are not likely to encounter any resistance from your child during this phase. In fact, you are most likely to enjoy a few weeks of wonderful results. He is on top of everything and is so happy to be meeting your expectations and to be involved. He loves his calendar pages and timers. He loves review meetings and he loves feeling and being accountable and responsible. With the occasional hiccup, he will most likely be 100% successful at managing his mornings from the start. Very cool! You'll be so happy you chose this program. All the time and effort to clarify your parenting purpose and to implement the Morning Peacemaker will seem worth it.

Your child's performance and thoughts tend to be objective early on, but slowly change to include a bit of subjective opinion and minor questions of reasons why things are the way they are. Behavior changes subtly at first, but you will notice an increase in complexity as he begins to use his own judgment and settles in. Here is an example:

It's the third week using the program and he has been performing at or near 100% success. The only issues have been minor—an overlooked task or rushing through marking his calendar page. Of late you notice him lingering in bed longer and longer each morning. With increasing anxiety you've watched this apparent gradual decline in enthusiasm for the program and notice his frustration growing as he needs to scramble at the last minute to complete his tasks.

On this day he has waited just a tad too long, and it's meant that he didn't have time to make his bed. He wants to earn his bonus pay and tells you it isn't fair that he ran out of time. He doesn't remember the leisure time he had in bed reading.

This is an example of his subjective opinion and judgment in action. He used to jump out of bed doing all his tasks within the first few snooze settings. This left a large amount of time for play before the morning's end. At first that extra time was great, but he gradually became restless and bored. He decided to use some of that extra time up front, lingering in bed rather than jumping right into action. Today he found the limit and it cost him a day's bonus. Better to have lost a dollar today than to have lost a job as an adult because he shows up late for work. Does the connection to adult employment help you find the right action to take now? Does it help you remain positive even in the face of apparent failure? You bet it does!

Slipping/Testing Phase

From the second month through the fourth or fifth, your child will be swinging on the pendulum between conscious and unconscious—competence and incompetence. Mixed in with the swings is a bit of budding independence, trying to figure out the lay of the land. Mistakes in this phase can be a genuine slip into unconscious incompetence or a conscious decision to be incompetent. I'll give you an example:

At the end of the morning your child marks his calendar page, indicating that he has brushed his teeth. You catch a whiff of his breath and know otherwise. You ask him in a nonjudgmental and supportive manor about his teeth and he confesses that he actually did not brush. Was he being consciously incompetent, not wanting to brush but marking his page as though he had been hoping you wouldn't notice? Was he so used to brushing and marking his calendar page complete that he didn't really pay attention as he marked his page, meaning a slip into unconscious incompetence?

> *Genius is the capacity for seeing relationships where lesser men see none. –William James*

It is complicated for both of you trying to identify a natural swing from a clash with old programming or a bit of muscle flexing. A clash or power play can bring back bad memories of failed efforts in the past, making a natural swing hard to differentiate. You may question whether this program is working or be tempted to "help" your child a little or give up entirely, feeling justified that you tried and the program failed you. It is important to keep your sights on the long-term objectives and the real lessons you're teaching. The only way you can get where you want to be is to stay focused and to keep going.

You're probably wondering how to respond to the situation above. Is there a different response depending on his intent? No, you are focused on the long-term objective and, therefore, your response is consistent. You calmly tell him that brushing his teeth is not optional; it must be done every day because it's important to maintain health and to show respect for yourself and others. Point out that the control he has over his results is whether to brush within the morning parameters and receive bonus pay or to brush after, forfeiting his bonus. You see, regardless of his intent, your answer is the same: positive and supportive reinforcement of the long-term objective.

Keep in mind: Your child will continue to flex his newly found muscles here and there, trying to push your buttons. He's figuring out how much control he has, which is an excellent thing! How else can he be accountable for his life if he doesn't learn how to take control of it, right? Unfortunately, neither one of you knows just how much control is available to him, so the button-pushing and muscle-flexing is necessary. It's all trial and error because you and he will only know he's taken too much control when he has actually done so. Without keeping your focus on what's really going on behind the scenes, this phase can be downright awful.

Though you might be ready for him to take control of making his bed and brushing his teeth, you might not be ready for him to question why he should. Questioning why tests the reasoning for the tasks, and this is a necessary step if he is to come to grips with independence. Through this process he will find his own good reasons why these things need to be done, reasons that feel good to him in his unique way of looking at the world. Because you've taken the time to think through everything in advance and have a simple and valid reason for all he is asked to do, his growth is inevitable. Here is another example:

It's Saturday and he isn't going out until later in the afternoon. He consciously decides not to brush his hair because it seems silly to brush in the morning when no one will see him until the afternoon. At the end of the morning he marks his page, showing he didn't brush his hair, and tells you why. To him it is reasonable; you may even find some merit to his thoughts. So what do you do? Think a moment: Is his hair really the issue or is it an example of something bigger? It's not unusual to find yourself in the position of having to do a task that you find unreasonable or silly. How many men would agree that wearing a necktie at work has no merit? How often will your child think his homework is silly or unreasonable? The examples of bigger lessons, while in themselves unimportant, are lessons that can only be learned in their examples. Your response should focus on the need for people to stick to the bargains they make; he expects you to uphold your end and you expect the same in return. That's not to say that the deal must remain as it is forever; he can introduce a change at any review meeting, but not until then. Remember, there are no mid-week discussions about changing the deal. Encourage him by reinforcing your priority to always find the right blend of needs and desires so that everyone can be happy.

> *Freedom to differ is not limited to things that do not offer much. That would be a mere shadow of freedom. The test of its substance is the right to differ as to things that touch the heart of the existing order.*
> *–Abraham Lincoln*

Be patient and allow him to poke around a bit about his tasks, and be prepared for him to start poking around about other things, too. The effects of the Morning Peacemaker won't be limited just to the morning. It is in this Slipping and Testing phase that you begin to notice the spreading of your child's wings. He may question why he has to do his homework at the usual time of day versus some other time. Though he may have asked that question in the past, now it will be asked from his newly found position of power. Stay calm, have good responses and be open to other ideas he has.

You never know when he will truly come up with a better way of doing something.

Please keep in mind that the arbitrary "because I said so" won't support the long-term objectives you have. Your child needs to understand for himself why these things are required, even though he doesn't want to do them. It might take a few struggles for him to find the right answers. Keep your focus! You don't want him to limit his feelings of accountability, responsibility, self-control and confidence just to the morning. You're looking for these big things to filter all the way through his being so that he will feel equally accountable for his homework, eating habits, behavior with others, etc. It stands to reason that he will need to question and flex and test things all the way through his life. Hopefully, he will agree 100% with everything you think; but it's likely he will have his own twist on at least a few things. Keep in mind that, while he might have your eyes, he is totally unique. How cool is that? Very cool if you can stand back and recognize what is really happening.

ROUTINE PHASE

Congratulations! You've made it to the new "normal" for your home and it includes an independent child with whom you have a peaceful relationship. Beginning around the fifth month using the program, your child quietly goes about his tasks each day. He no longer clings to the calendar pages or the timers; he sees them as tools, not crutches. (Cha-ching!) His inner confidence has flowed out to other parts of the day. In the afternoon, his homework gets done with less dependence on you and, though he may grumble, he's resigned himself to the fact that homework is a necessary evil. (Payday!) He decides on his own when a shower is needed—well, occasionally, anyway. (Bonus!) He hands you an Internet address that has funny comics he likes so you'll be able to make his pages even more meaningful to him. (Right on!) He asks you to put "Remember your trumpet" on his Thursday calendar pages so every Thursday he's got a built-in reminder. He is acting on his own behalf in many, many ways. Let me tell you how freeing this is! He is now relieving you of the pressure to make him happy and successful. He is taking action in advance to set up his success! (Yes!)

> *The way I look at it, if you want the rainbow, you gotta put up with the rain.*
> *–Dolly Parton*

The Routine Phase is not without some challenges, but they are small blips on the screen—the occasional forgetfulness or the sleeping late that we all have done and regretted. There can even be a string of blips, but these are more an indication of your child's growth and distraction in other areas than a return to his dependence on you. Once the distraction is over, things are smooth again. You've done your job well.

ONE DAY AT A TIME

I know the price of success: dedication, hard work and an unremitting devotion to the things you want to see happen.

–Frank Lloyd Wright

The most changes in the program occur within the first few months. This is the time of discovery, testing and learning from the inevitable mistakes. As the first few weeks pass, strategies that initially worked may need tweaking or total revision. You'll start with a great deal of interest and positive results that flow into a time of slipping and testing. From there, as you are consistent and supportive and zipped lipped, your child will move from the slipping/testing into a comfortable place where he is accountable—truly accountable. He will be successful more often than not but there will be days when something is forgotten. Now, when he forgets something, the blame game is gone and he faces his consequences with confidence and learns a lesson of his own making.

> *Instead of thinking about where you are, think about where you want to be. It takes twenty years of hard work to become an overnight success.*
>
> *–Unknown*

When this occurs for the first time and you witness the subtle change in attitude, you will be truly overjoyed. You will want to call everyone you know and tell them that your son forgot his trumpet for school and actually said, "Oh man, I can't believe I forgot my trumpet. I'll just have to make it up at my next lesson." What a far cry from, "You forgot to give me my trumpet! It's all your fault and my teacher is gonna be really mad. You have to go back and bring it to me or else I'm gonna get in trouble."

Someone who has experienced the benefits of being a Peacemaker Parent will want to pop the champagne cork right along with you. The moment ranks up there with the first time he "made it" to the potty or the first day of kindergarten. It ranks so high because it is your first glimpse of the adult he is to become. It's your first encounter with that new person who is no longer a complete dependent. But unlike the tears you might have shed over the first day of school, you will be relieved and thankful. You will look to the future, feeling that he will really be okay without you one day. You'll feel like the awesome parent you are, and that deserves a celebration!

In the event you call someone to share in your triumph and she hasn't yet discovered *The Peacemaker Parent*, she might not be able to appreciate the victory. She may still be limiting her view to the short-term results, thinking only that your child forgot his trumpet. You and I now understand that the trumpet isn't the thing and so, for your friend's sake, just tell her you're happy; and then, right after you hang up the phone, mail her a copy of this book! If she's ready to do what it takes to become a Peacemaker Parent, you may very well get a similar phone call from her within the next few months.

APPENDIX

Creating the Calendar Page

For those of us with limited computer skills, or who are at all hesitant about creating the calendar pages, you can stop worrying. Below is a walk-through of the process. I've created these instructions in two ways: a wordy-descriptive version and a picture-speaks-a-thousand-words version. Feel free to reach out for help at *www.Peacemaker-Coach.com*.

THE WORDY-DESCRIPTIVE VERSION

STEP 1—OPEN MICROSOFT POWERPOINT

Your goal is to open to a blank page design. Though you can also create the calendar page in Microsoft Word or in Excel, I recommend PowerPoint or, for Mac users, Pages, because it provides a simple-yet-flexible platform for both text and graphics. The slides you create in PowerPoint or Pages are the calendar pages for your child. I am a PC user, so my instructions are for PowerPoint 2007 and 2010.

To open PowerPoint, right-click on the PowerPoint icon. Alternatively, you can right-click the START button, then right-click PROGRAMS in the pull-down menu, and then right-click PowerPoint. Depending on the version of PowerPoint you're using, it will either open to a text box asking how you want to create your new presentation (choose BLANK for the first one), or it will open with a default slide design, "Office Theme." If the program opens to the default, 2010 users are all set. If using version 2007, select GETTING STARTED, and then NEW PRESENTATION. Right-click on BLANK PRESENTATION.

STEP 2—CHOOSE A SLIDE LAYOUT

Choose a format that will allow both text and images. Images may be inserted anywhere on the page, regardless of the layout you choose. In the beginning, though, it will be easier to use a layout that specifies the location of text and images. The boxes that mark the location for the text and images within a slide are called placeholders. The layout I recommend positions the title placeholder at the top, the text placeholder on the left side and the image placeholder on the right.

Click to add title

• Click to add text

Double click to add clip art

2007: To choose a layout, select from the options automatically displayed or right-click on the FORMAT tab at the top of your computer screen/browser. Choose LAYOUT and make your selection. Scroll down to TEXT AND CONTENT LAYOUTS for your first try.

2010: The default layout is automatically loaded.

STEP 3—CHOOSE A SLIDE DESIGN

Your goal is to make the page look interesting to your child. The most important aspects of the calendar page are your child's image and the tasks. K.I.S.S. it—that is, keep it so simple, especially in the beginning. Too many design graphics at first will distract your child. In this case, less is more. I encourage you to keep the blank design and only insert one image of your child for the first few months. After he and you have gotten used to the program, you can add other images to support ideas or add to the humor of the page.

7:30   October 13, 2009   8:30

• Click to add text

Double click to add clip art

2007: Right-click the FORMAT tab at the very top of your computer screen/ browser and select SLIDE LAYOUT. Right-click on SLIDE DESIGN and scroll down to find one that suits your need.

Click to add title

Click to add subtitle

2010: Right-click LAYOUT located in the slides section of the ribbon. From the options displayed right-click TWO CONTENT.

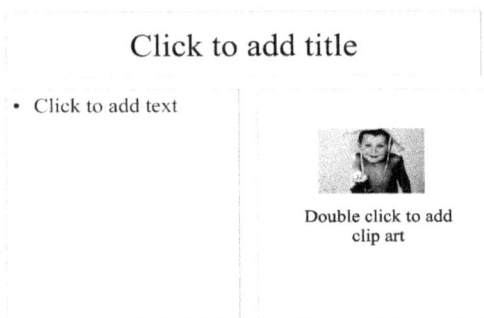

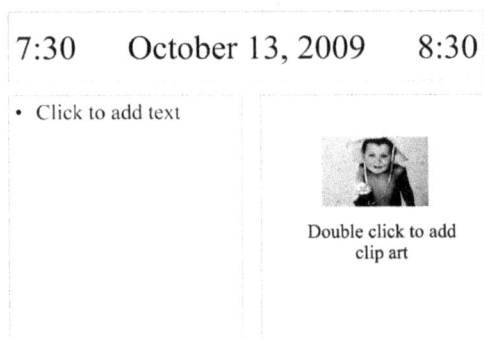

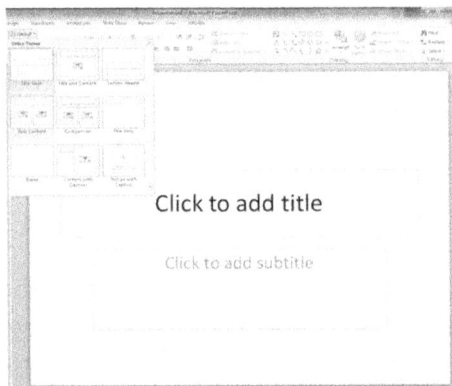

STEP 4—ADD DATE AND START/END TIMES IN THE TITLE PLACEHOLDER

Center the day of the week and the date between the morning start and end times. The text font will automatically be a large size, which works great for a plain slide layout. Font refers to the size and style of letters and numbers. If you use a slide design that decreases the available input area for the Title placeholder, you may need to either decrease the font size of the text or increase the area size for the Title placeholder.

To decrease the font size, highlight the words you want to change.

2007: Right-click FORMAT at the top of the computer screen/browser. Select FONT, right-click the new font size and click OK. Repeat, if needed, until you find the right fit.

2010: Right-click the pull-down font size menu located in the font section of the ribbon.

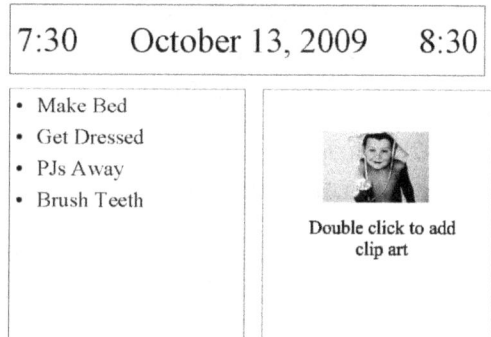

7:30	October 13, 2009	8:30

- Make Bed
- Get Dressed
- PJs Away
- Brush Teeth

Double click to add clip art

To increase the Title placeholder size, right-click inside the Title placeholder to highlight the placeholder outlines. Move the cursor to any corner of the placeholder box until you see a ray icon (a short line with arrows at each end, pointing in opposite directions). Right-click your mouse and hold it down as you drag the box into the shape/size you need. Release the mouse to set the new shape.

STEP 5—ADD TASKS TO TEXT PLACEHOLDER

2007: Click inside the Text placeholder and type in the tasks.

2010: Right-click the words "Click to add text" in the left content box and begin typing.

The Text placeholder will automatically assign a bullet point for each entry. You can automatically create the check-off box by formatting the bullets.

7:30	October 13, 2009	8:30

- Make Bed
- Get Dressed
- PJs Away
- Brush Teeth

2007: Click FORMAT at the top of your computer screen/browser. Select BULLETS AND NUMBERING. Then select BULLETED.

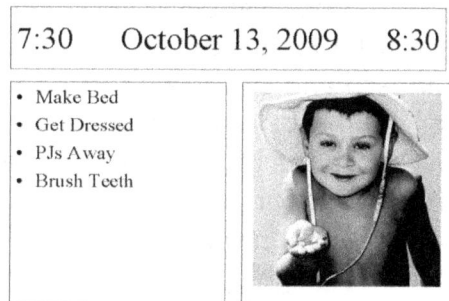

2010: Click the pull-down bullet options menu located in the paragraph section of the ribbon.

You'll find a few styles of bullets from which to choose. Pick one that your child will easily recognize as the right place to mark off a completed task. Try to keep each task name short so that it fits on one line within the Text placeholder.

Step 6—Add Image To Image Placeholder

Insert an image of your child that will draw his or her positive attention to the calendar page. You may use digital photos from your camera or scanned photos and artwork downloaded to your computer. You can even use comics and Clip Art!

2007 and 2010: Click the "mountain picture" icon and navigate through your computer files to locate an image of your child.

To streamline calendar page creation and organize the images you'll use, create a separate folder on your computer's hard drive. Doing so prevents unintended duplication.

Step 7—Save The Presentation

After you've created the first calendar page, create a new folder to house all the calendar pages for the month. To do this, right-click FILE at the top of the screen/browser, then right-click SAVE AS. Create a new folder by right-clicking the icon that looks like a closed file folder. Name the folder with your child's name and the month—for example "Michael October 2009." The name of the folder now appears in the SAVE AS text box. Right-click SAVE at the bottom left, and you've done it! On Monday, October 12, you'll open the MICHAEL OCTOBER 2009 presentation folder, double right-click TUE 13 and print. It's that simple! After creating a few pages, you'll be a pro.

With one calendar page created, you can streamline the process by using it as a template for the other pages that month. Since tasks should all be standard and consistently needed, the task list won't require much change. For the most part, only the main image of your child and the date change. To change the image, left-click on the image and right-click CUT. Follow the instructions for Step 6 above and poof, it's changed. To change the date, hold the right mouse button down as you drag the curser over the old information to highlight the text. Type over with the new information and save the new page "WED 14." Voilà!

As you get comfortable, begin to add graphics to the edges of the calendar pages. This will help to keep your child's interest high. One month your child may be interested in Star Wars, the next month it's swimming. With a little effort on your part at the beginning of the month, you can select a few background images that support your child's new interests. It is also an opportunity for you to promote positive messages that you want him or her to absorb. Pictures of friendship, achievement or community are easily added to reinforce a positive self-image and connections to broader messages, and these are free, using Microsoft Clip Art Online. By playing around with the basic steps in PowerPoint, Pages and Clip Art, you'll be able to create attention-grabbing calendar pages that support your child as he or she becomes independent. You can get fancy; just remember—fancy is great as long as the message isn't lost.

The Picture-Is-Worth-A-Thousand-Words Version

SELECT LAYOUT

- After Opening PowerPoint:

2007: Select a predesigned template from the options shown on the right side of your computer screen.

Left-click the design you like and APPLY to the slide.

2010: Click LAYOUT then TWO CONTENT

ADD TIME AND DAY

2007 AND 2010: Right-click inside the Title placeholder and type the start time, day and date, and end time.

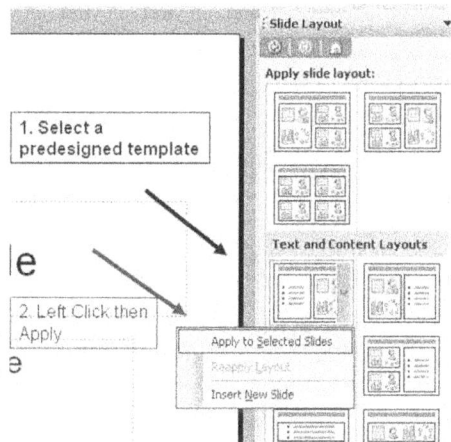

1. Select a predesigned template

2. Left Click then Apply

Slide Layout

Apply slide layout:

Text and Content Layouts

Apply to Selected Slides
Reapply Layout
Insert New Slide

Click to add title

Click to add subtitle

| 7:30 | Monday 4/3/06 | 8:30 |

• Click to add text | Right click Title Placeholder then type start time, day and date, and end time

ADD TASKS

7:30   Monday 4/3/06   8:30

2007: Right-click inside the Text placeholder and type in the tasks. The bullets will automatically be assigned as dots.

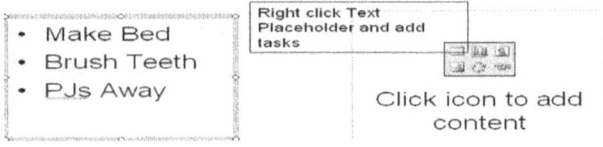

- Make Bed
- Brush Teeth
- PJs Away

Right click Text Placeholder and add tasks

Click icon to add content

2010: Click on the words "Click to add text".

TO CHANGE THE SHAPE OF THE BULLET:

2007: Right-click FORMAT.

Right-click BULLETS AND NUMBERING.

I recommend using a bullet that gives your child a clear place to mark completed tasks.

Left-click on the style you like.

Right-click OK.

2010: Click pull-down menu for bullet options located in paragraph section of the ribbon.

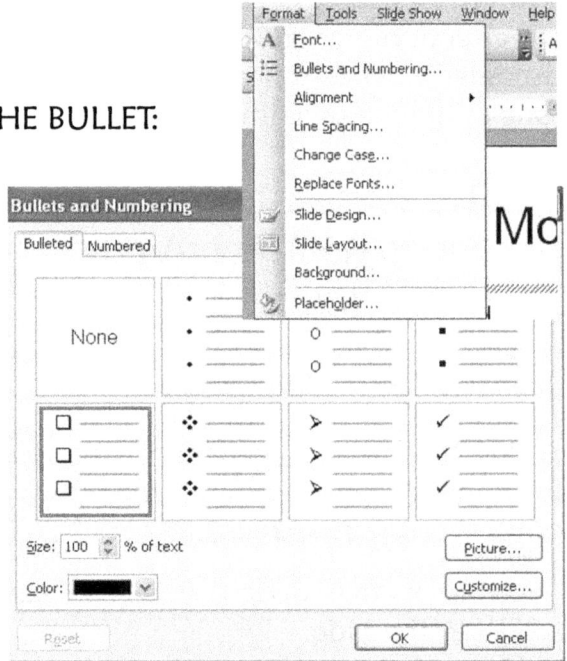

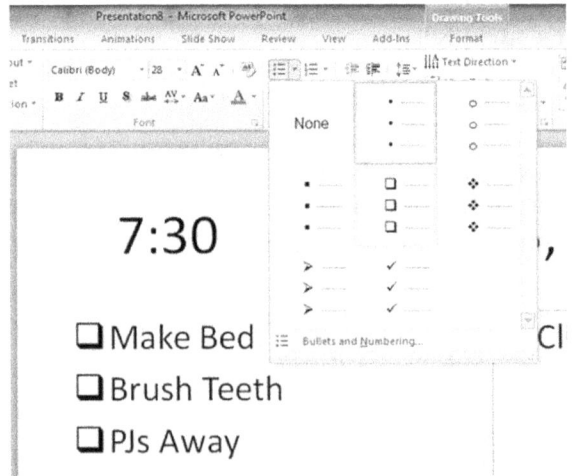

7:30

☐ Make Bed
☐ Brush Teeth
☐ PJs Away

INSERT PICTURE

2007 and 2010: Right-click on the graphic that looks like a mountain and sun.

Navigate your way to the folder that contains all the pictures you plan to use for this month's calendar pages. Double left-click the image to insert it onto the calendar page.

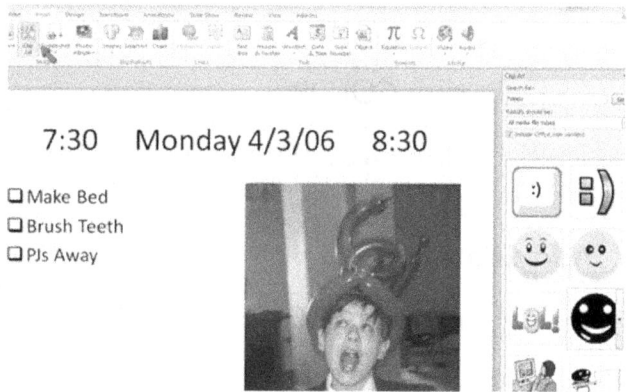

YOU'RE ALL DONE!

Congratulations! You've just created your first basic calendar page. See, it's not so tough; and the more you do it, the easier it becomes. I can create basic calendar pages for both boys for an entire month in less than 30 minutes. I know that if I can do it, so can you.

7:30   Monday 4/3/06   8:30

- Make Bed
- Brush Teeth
- PJs Away

OPTIONAL FANCY THINGS

After you've created a few calendar pages, you may decide that a couple bells and whistles would be nice. Below are three ways to add some flare. Caution: More is not more. Adding too many fancy things can overwhelm your child, *so less is more here.*

Add Color to Text

1. Highlight the text.

2. Right-click FORMAT.

3. Right-click FONT.

4. Right-click COLOR.

5. Right-click OK.

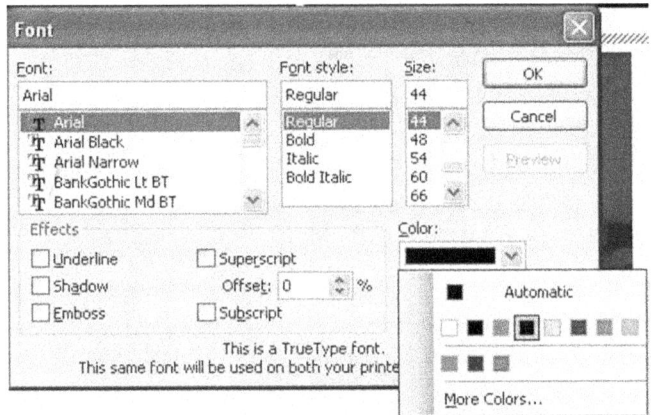

Add Clip Art

1. Right-click INSERT.

2. Right-click PICTURE.

3. Right-click CLIP ART.

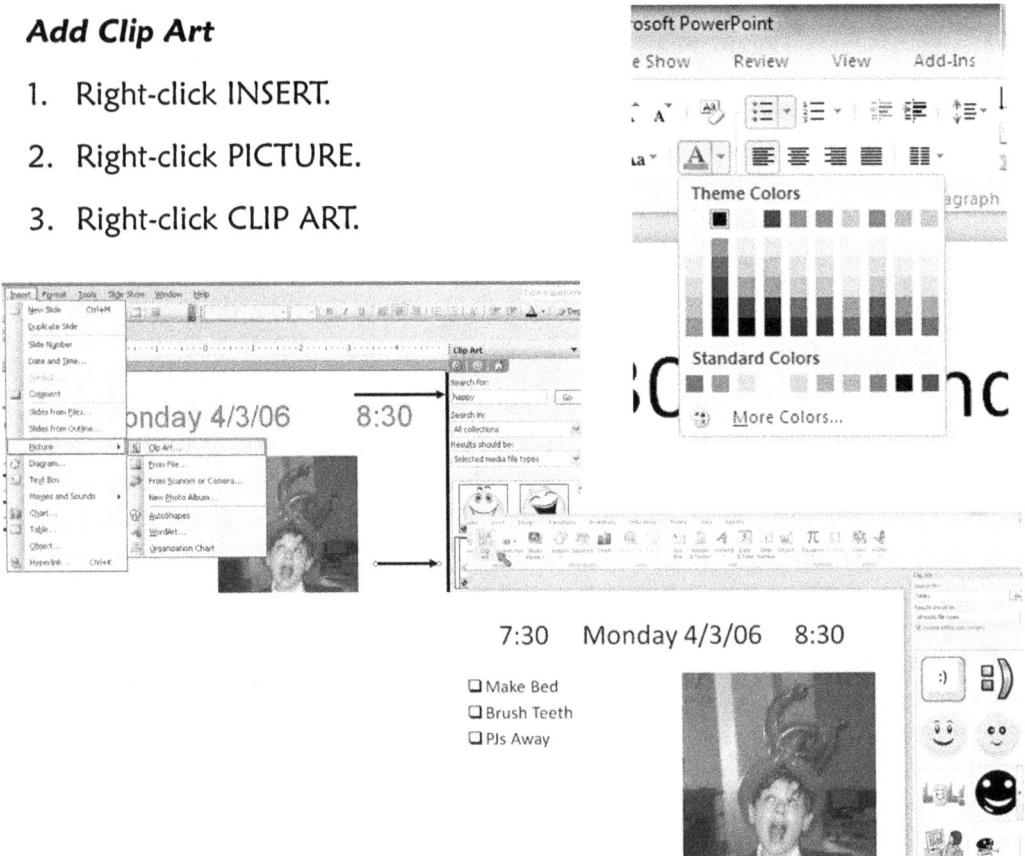

Add Special Message

1.   Right-click INSERT.

2.   Right-click PICTURE.

3.   Right-click WORD ART.

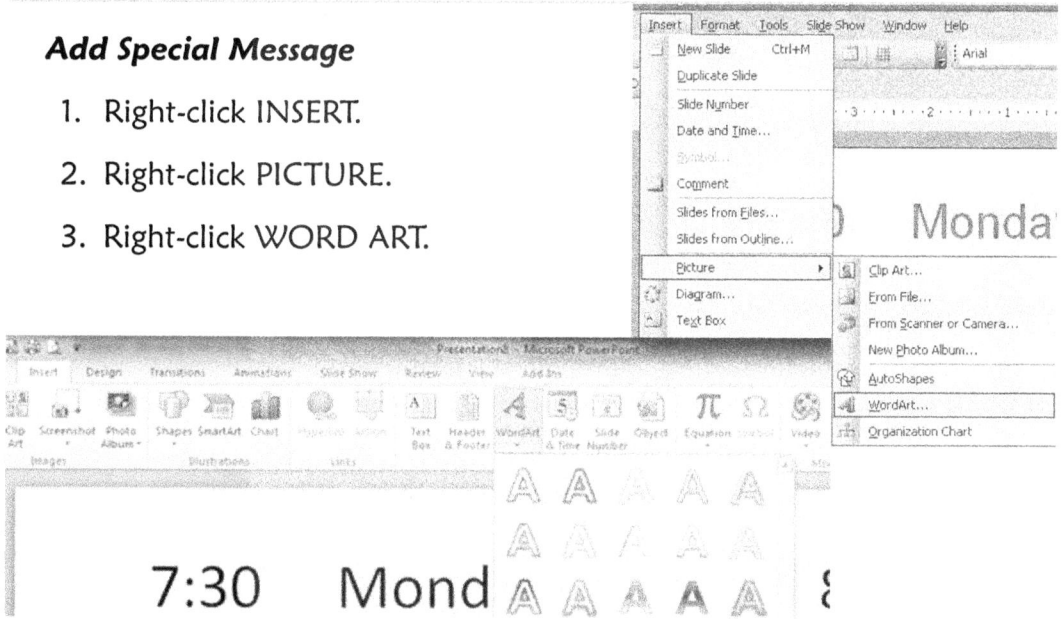

THE FINISHED PAGE

You've entered the time/day and changed the color of the text. You've listed the tasks to be completed and changed the style of the bullets to allow for a check-off. You've added a picture of your child and even decorated the page with clip art and a special message. Well Done!

7:30   Monday 4/3/06   8:30

❑ Make Bed
❑ Brush Teeth
❑ PJs Away

I Love You!

ABOUT THE AUTHOR

Lorraine Esposito is a life coach and author. She has been featured in broadcast, print and online media and is a public speaker regarding personal leadership and empowered parenting to community and school-based audiences. Lorraine lives in New York with her husband and two sons.

www.ingramcontent.com/pod-product-compliance
Lightning Source LLC
Chambersburg PA
CBHW080935040426
42443CB00015B/3414